The First European Elections

THE FIRST EUROPEAN ELECTIONS

A Handbook and Guide

**Chris Cook and
Mary Francis**

© Chris Cook, 1979

First published 1979 by
THE MACMILLAN PRESS LTD
London and Basingstoke

Associated companies in *Delhi Dublin
Hong Kong Johannesburg Lagos Melbourne
New York Singapore and Tokyo*

British Library Cataloguing in Publication Data

Cook, Chris
    The first European elections.
    1. European Parliament — Elections
    I. Title   II. Francis, Mary
    324',21   JN36

83569

324·4
Coo
①

ISBN 0—333—26574—2
ISBN 0—333—26575—0 Pbk

Printed in Great Britain by
Billing & Sons Limited, Guildford, London and Worcester

Acknowledgements

This book owes a considerable debt to a variety of individuals and organisations. Most particularly I must thank my co-author, Mary Francis of Nuffield College, Oxford, whose detailed specialist knowledge of this subject and willing collaboration in this book have been invaluable. I have relied heavily on the advice and friendship of Dr. Alan Sked of the London School of Economics for the diplomatic background of British membership of the Community. He has generously given permission to quote extracts from his forthcoming study of post-war British politics. I must also thank Anne Stevens and Philip Jones for their help and assistance, most particularly over the intricacies of the European Parliament and the details of the political parties fighting the elections. The staff of the London offices of the European Commission and European Parliament have given generously of their time. A special debt is due to the Warden and Fellows of Nuffield College, Oxford and in particular to Clive Payne and the staff of the computing unit. At Macmillan, my thanks are due to Anne-Lucie Norton and Shaie Selzer for their encouragement and help. Finally I must give my warm thanks to John Paxton at whose suggestion I undertook the compilation of this book. The chronology of events is reproduced with permission from his invaluable *Dictionary of the European Economic Community*.

It is hoped to make this handbook a regular feature of future European Elections. The author and publishers will welcome suggestions for additional topics to be included for the 1984 edition.

Chris Cook
1 January 1979

Contents

Contents

Contents

List of Tables

List of Illustrations

Abbreviations

CAP	Common Agricultural Policy
EBU	European Broadcasting Union
EDC	European Defence Community
EEC	European Economic Community
EP	European Parliament
LAGER	Liberal Action Group for Electoral Reform
MP	Member of Parliament
NATO	North Atlantic Treaty Organisation
OEEC	Organisation for European Economic Cooperation
ORC	Opinion Research Centre
PC	Plaid Cymru
PR	Proportional Representation
SDLP	Social Democratic and Labour Party
SNP	Scottish National Party
STV	Single Transferable Vote
UK	United Kingdom
UN	United Nations
UUUC	United Ulster Unionist Council

Chapter 1

The Background to British Entry into Europe

Chronology of Main Events 1945–1973

19 Sept	*1946*	Winston Churchill, in a speech at Zurich, urges Franco-German reconciliation with 'a kind of United States of Europe'.
5 June	*1947*	General Marshall proposes American aid to stimulate recovery in Europe.
29 Oct	*1947*	Creation of Benelux — economic union of Belgium, Luxembourg and the Netherlands.
16 April	*1948*	Convention for European Economic Co-operation signed — the birth of OEEC.
5 May	*1949*	Statute of the Council of Europe signed.
9 May	*1950*	Robert Schuman makes his historic proposal to place French and German coal and steel under a common Authority.
18 April	*1951*	The Treaty setting up the European Coal and Steel Community (ECSC) is signed in Paris.
10 Feb	*1953*	ECSC common market for coal, iron ore, and scrap is opened.
1 May	*1953*	ECSC common market for steel is opened.
1-3 June	*1955*	Messina Conference: the Foreign Ministers of the Community's member states propose further steps towards full integration in Europe.
25 March	*1957*	Signature of the Rome Treaties setting up the Common Market and Euratom.

1

1 Jan	*1958*	The Rome Treaties come into force: the Common Market and Euratom are established.
19-21 March	*1958*	First session of the European Parliament — Robert Schuman elected President.
1 Jan	*1959*	First tariff reductions and quota enlargements in the Common Market. Establishment of common market for nuclear materials.
20 Nov	*1959*	European Free Trade Association convention signed between Austria, Denmark, Norway, Portugal, Sweden, Switzerland and the United Kingdom.
9 July	*1961*	Greece signs association agreement with EEC (comes into force 1 Nov 1962).
1 Aug	*1961*	The Republic of Ireland applies for membership of the Common Market.
10 Aug	*1961*	The United Kingdom and Denmark request negotiations aiming at membership of the Common Market.
8 Nov	*1961*	Negotiations with the United Kingdom open in Brussels.
15 Dec	*1961*	The three neutrals, Austria, Sweden and Switzerland, apply for association with the Common Market.
30 April	*1962*	Norway requests negotiations for membership of the Common Market.
14 Jan	*1963*	President de Gaulle declares that the United Kingdom is not ready for Community membership.
29 Jan	*1963*	United Kingdom negotiations with Six broken off.
1 July	*1963*	Signature of Yaounde Convention, associating eighteen independent states in Africa and Madagascar with the Community for five years from 1 June 1964.

2

12 Sept	*1963*	Turkey signs association agreement with Community (comes into force 1 Dec 1964).
9 Dec	*1964*	First meeting of the Parliamentary Conference of members of European Parliament and parliamentarians from Yaounde associated states.
15 Dec	*1964*	Council adopts the Mansholt Plan for common prices for grains.
31 March	*1965*	Common Market Commission proposes that, as from 1 July 1967, all Community countries' import duties and levies be paid into Community budget and that powers of European Parliament be increased.
8 April	*1965*	Six sign treaty merging the Community Executives.
31 May	*1965*	Common Market Commission publishes first memorandum proposing lines of Community policy for regional development.
1 July	*1965*	Council fails to reach agreement by agreed deadline on financing common farm policy; French boycott of Community Institutions begins seven-month-long crisis.
26 July	*1965*	Council meets and conducts business without French representative present.
17 Jan	*1966*	Six foreign ministers meet in Luxembourg without Commission present and agree to resume full Community activity.
10 Nov	*1966*	United Kingdom Prime Minister Harold Wilson announces plans for 'a high-level approach' to the Six with intention of entering EEC.
11 May	*1967*	The United Kingdom lodges formal application for membership of the European Economic Community.

3

16 May	*1968*	Second de Gaulle veto on British application.
25 April	*1969*	General de Gaulle resigns as President of France.
2 Dec	*1969*	At a Summit Conference at The Hague the Community formally agree to open membership negotiations with the United Kingdom, Norway, Denmark and the Republic of Ireland on their applications of 1967.
29 June	*1970*	Talks begin in Luxembourg between the Six and the United Kingdom, Norway, Denmark and the Republic of Ireland.
23 June	*1971*	The Council of Ministers of the Community announces that agreement has been reached with the United Kingdom for the basis of the accession of the United Kingdom to the Communities.
11-13 July	*1971*	At a Ministerial-level negotiating session, agreement is reached on major outstanding issues: the transitional period for the United Kingdom; Commonwealth Sugar; Capital Movements; and the common commercial policy.
28 Oct	*1971*	Vote in the House of Commons on the motion 'That this House approves Her Majesty's Government's decision of principle to join the European Communities on the basis of the arrangements which have been negotiated'. The voting figures in the House of Commons were 356 for, 244 against, majority of 112; and in the House of Lords 451 for, 58 against, majority of 393.
22 Jan	*1972*	Treaty of Accession was signed in Brussels between the European Communities (France, Belgium, Germany, Italy, Luxembourg and the Netherlands) on the one side and the United Kingdom, Denmark, Norway and the Republic of Ireland on the other

4

side.

22 July	*1972*	EEC signs free trade agreements with Austria, Iceland, Portugal, Sweden and Switzerland.
26 Sept	*1972*	Rejection by Norway of full membership of EEC following a referendum.
31 Dec	*1972*	The United Kingdom and Denmark withdraw from EFTA.
1 Jan	*1973*	The United Kingdom, Irish Republic and Denmark join the Community.

On 1 January 1973, the United Kingdom, along with Denmark and Ireland formally joined the European Community. Over 25 years earlier, in January 1947, a United Europe Committee had been formed in London with Churchill as its Chairman. The quarter of a century between these two events constituted a period of lost opportunity for Britain. While a new united Europe was being created — symbolised by the signing of the Treaty of Rome in March 1957 by the six founder members of the EEC — Britain was playing no part in creating this new Europe. When, eventually, Britain applied for membership of the Community in 1961, it was only to be rebuffed by the de Gaulle veto. Since then, divisions over European entry have existed not only between the major parties but within them. The story of Britain's applications to join the Community, and the political controversy and debate that this has aroused, constitute the essential historical backcloth to the forthcoming direct elections.

The Idea of European Unity

The ideas of closer European unity — even the creation of a 'United States of Europe' — took root in the immediate post-1945 period.[1] A variety of impulses helped this move towards unity. Partly there was the desire to assert the interests of Europe in the face of the domination of the American and Soviet super-powers. There was also the urgent need to heal the deep wounds inflicted by the second world war. Last but not least, there was the political influence of such visionaries as the French economic planner, Jean Monnet. Even before the second world war, Monnet had been actively putting forward this ideal. In addition, the idea had also gained many adherents among the European underground resistance during the war. It was strongly reinforced, however, when Churchill at Zurich in September 1946 spoke of the need to create 'a kind of United States of Europe' based on Franco-German reconciliation. Churchill also advocated the establishment of a 'Council of Europe', although it seemed Britain was to be a 'friend and sponsor' rather than a member of it. In January 1947 the formation was announced of a United Europe Committee. This body aimed at the creation of a 'unified Europe' and Britain, it was declared, despite her special obligations to the Commonwealth was to play a full and active part in it. In July the same year a French committee was formed and in December, British, French, Belgian and Dutch members set up an International Committee for a United Europe, chaired by Churchill's son-in-law, Duncan Sandys. The scenario seemed ripe therefore, for a 'Congress of Europe' to be held.

The Hague Conference

This duly met at The Hague in May 1948. Such leading Conservatives as Eden and Macmillan attended, along with other Conservative MPs. So too did a few Labour members. Delegations were present from other European countries — including, significantly, Germany. In addition, there were representatives-in-exile from the now Communist-dominated East European states. The main speaker at the Congress was Churchill who delivered a very moving speech full of somewhat vague rhetoric. His vision seemed to be one of three regional councils dominating world affairs: one based on the Soviet Union; the Council of Europe 'including Great Britain joined with her Empire and Commonwealth'; and one in the Western Hemisphere with which Britain would also be linked through Canada.[2] As well as Churchill's woolly oratory, there was the more precise resolution of the Congress to create a European economic and political union and its call for a European Assembly to be chosen from the parliaments of the member states. Despite their vagueness Churchill and his Conservative colleagues had succeeded in giving the impression that their party stood for a united Europe. From the Labour viewpoint, on the other hand, the Attlee Government had adopted a fairly sceptical attitude towards the question of a federal Europe. It seemed that, as far as Labour was concerned, Britain was still a world power.

Her links with the Commonwealth and America still meant more than any ties she might have with the Continent. Australia and New Zealand were nearer to most British hearts than the countries which had so recently been our enemies. Labour appeared to assume that the ideal of a United Europe was for those who had suffered defeat in war. Their 'national pride' had been broken whereas that of Great Britain had not. The Labour Government, therefore, did not encourage its members to visit The Hague and Bevin replied to the Hague Conference resolutions unencouragingly.

Bevin's reply reflected the attitude of most of the party leadership. Labour's leaders, in fact, had little inclination to become involved with European integration. Indeed, they made this only too clear, most particularly in their dealings with the French. Thus the French suggestion to set up a European Customs Union was swiftly put aside. Likewise the powers demanded by the French for the Secretariat of the OEEC were significantly scaled down by the British.

In a sense, perhaps it can be argued that Bevin's stance turned not so much on matters of national pride and prejudice than on the question of priorities. Bevin was prepared to give some thought to the longterm possibility of a more integrated form of Europe, but in the short term his first priority was to secure the adequate defence of Europe, which clearly meant a close involvement with the United States. Bevin was thus much more interested in strengthening Europe's links with Amerca than in fostering European cooperation for the sake of cooperation. Even more importantly, since neither Germany nor Italy had armies, and that of France was still untried, there was perhaps even more reason for his scepticism.[3]

In addition, Bevin knew that American cooperation was much more likely to be forthcoming if Britain and France were seen to be cooperating first, hence Bevin's enthusiastic response to the proposals for an Anglo-French Treaty of Alliance which was to last for fifty years. This treaty was signed at Dunkirk in the following year.

Western Union

The same motive in Bevin's diplomacy was to be seen one year later when the Benelux countries — Belgium, Holland and Luxembourg — were, through the Brussels Treaty of March

7

1948, brought into a system of European defence.

Gradually the Western Union (as the Brussels Treaty was known) built up a military infrastructure. It met in Paris to establish a permanent organisation under its own authority with headquarters at Fontainebleau as well as a Chiefs of Staff Committee under the leadership of Field-Marshal Montgomery.

The more federalist-inclined European politicians who had been involved in the creation of European Union were determined to make the result really live up to the name. The French in particular were keen that more than just a common military structure should be the final outcome of the treaty. Encouraged by the favourable European sentiment which had been only too apparent at The Hague Congress that year, they persuaded the Ministerial Council of the Western Union, to set up a committee on European Union under the chairmanship of Herriot (then President of the French National Assembly). This was duly established, but its efforts were soon deadlocked by British opposition to the proposed creation of a European Assembly. However a compromise was reached in 1949 (by which time five more states had signed the Brussels Treaty) according to which a Council of Europe was to be created consisting of the Ministerial Council and a 'Consultative Assembly' of parliamentarians. Its aims were left distinctly vague: 'to achieve a greater unity between its members for the purpose of safeguarding and realising the ideals and principles which are their common heritage and facilitating their economic and social progress.' Great Britain had thus succeeded in rendering the Council of Europe fairly harmless, not least by the complicated Constitution and voting procedure of the Council.

European Defence

The next stage in the story of European unification took place against a very different backcloth. This time it was centred on the problem of Germany and the Russian blockade of Berlin. Given the seeming Soviet threat to Western Europe, and the series of Communist victories in Korea, clearly West German morale had to be bolstered. It was against this background that Adenauer proposed the establishment of a West German Federal Police Force consisting of 150,000 men. Adenauer also gave his approval to a speech made at this time by Winston Churchill who suggested the creation of a European Army. Churchill had made this speech without consulting Bevin and in it he proposed that the army should include German troops. Bevin did not like the plan, nor did the French and German Socialists. In September 1950, the Foreign Ministers of Britain, France and the United States met to discuss the German question. Many possible solutions were discussed. Eventually, a compromise was reached which temporarily shelved the question of West German military participation. The defence of Western Europe would be provided for by an integrated NATO army operating under a centralised command structure with an American supreme commander. Eisenhower was eventually given this job in January 1951 and America committed more troops to the defence of Western Europe. The result was yet another success for Bevin, for despite its supranational elements, NATO represented a pragmatic Atlanticist advance rather than a concession to European federalism.

The European Coal and Steel Community

After Bevin's successes in thwarting the European Federalists, it was now their opportunity to turn the tables on Britain and — in so doing — pave the way towards the eventual establishment of the Common Market. Thwarted by Britain over the matter of the constitution of the Council of Europe, they were determined that British nationalism should not again sabotage their plans. The issue which they chose was the proposed creation in May 1950 of a European Coal and Steel Community. The idea had first taken root, not surprisingly, in the fertile mind of Jean Monnet and was promoted politically and diplomatically by the French Foreign Minister, Robert Schuman. Both Monnet and Schuman wanted to find a solution to the German problem. Both were also committed to the ideal of a federalist Europe. Since it was clear that Germany would in the long term recover from her defeat, they now sought to marry idealism with realism and to absorb a potentially powerful Germany within the confines of a supra-national framework. Thus in May 1950 the 'Schuman Plan' was announced. France and Germany were both to place the control of their coal and steel production under the aegis of a single High Authority; other countries could adhere to the scheme if they wished and in this way a very important step could be taken towards European integration.

Neither the timing nor the nature of the announcement of the Schuman Plan had been calculated to win British sympathy or support. Britain had not been consulted beforehand. The Labour government was certain to disapprove strongly of the supra-nationalist implications of the scheme. And the whole scheme came at a time when British iron and steel were in the process of being nationalised. This new project threatened to reopen a debate which seemed to be almost over. For what was the point of nationalisation if control of the industries which had just been nationalised would pass immediately into foreign hands. As Alan Sked has written 'British socialists had not just conquered the commanding heights to surrender them to German capitalists. It was little wonder, therefore, that the latest federalist proposals were received with less than enthusiasm in London. Finally the fact that the American Secretary of State, Dean Acheson, had privately been warned of the scheme in advance and later accorded it his warm and wholehearted support led Bevin to believe that he was being made the victim of a diplomatic plot.' Thus Attlee stated that the scheme would require 'detailed study and consideration'. He sympathised with attempts to resolve Franco-German differences but could not commit his government to support the scheme immediately. The French, however, were determined to retain the diplomatic initiative, and in May 1950 they invited Britain, Italy and the Benelux countries to enter into negotiations on the plan. Skilfully, the French placed upon these discussions the condition that the principle of supra-nationalism should be accepted in advance. For Britain, this was unacceptable. But British objections were rejected and the proposed discussions were held without her. The outcome was the treaty signed in April 1951 which established the European Coal and Steel Community. Recognising the importance of what had happened, Great Britain now adopted a conciliatory attitude towards the newly-established body and at the end of November 1951 appointed a permanent delegation to the High Authority. But Britain had missed out on one of the most important milestones on the road to European cooperation.

The Birth of the Common Market

In 1951 the Conservatives returned to power in Britain. Led by Churchill until 1955, and with Eden as his successor in that year, their period in office saw few changes in Britain's attitudes to Europe. The protracted discussions over the proposed European Defence Community in 1952 had showed that Churchill was no more willing than Bevin had been to surrender British sovereignty. This British attitude to Europe remained the same throughout the 1950s. As Sked has written: 'Britain's concern with her Commonwealth and Empire, with transatlantic relations and with her independent nuclear deterrent meant that the British public had even less regard for what was happening in Europe than it usually had.'[4] It was against this background that the far-reaching events that were to give birth to the Common Market took place.[5]

The suggestion of a 'European Common Market' was presented in a memorandum of the Benelux governments to the governments of France, Germany and Italy on 20 May 1955. On 2 June the Foreign Ministers of the Six met at Messina in Italy to consider the proposal. At this meeting an intergovernmental committee was established under Paul-Henri Spaak, the Belgian Foreign Minister, to prepare a detailed plan. In spring 1956 it submitted a report. The drafting of the treaties which established the European Economic Community and Euratom then followed. These were signed in Rome in March 1957 and ratified by the Six in the following months. They took effect from 1 January 1958. France, on this occasion, was well satisfied. The Common Market was to be a common market not merely for industrial goods but also for agricultural produce.

The speed with which these events took place left Britain somewhat stunned. Ever since the fiasco of the EDC, Britain had poured scorn on the European federalist movement and did not expect another initiative to come from it so soon. The federalists, however, determined to make up for their defeat over the EDC, had advanced on a new front very quickly. Britain was certainly caught off guard, although there had been no attempt, as in the case of the Schuman Plan, to exclude Britain from the start by insisting on a supra-nationalist commitment in advance. Indeed, at the Messina conference, Britain was invited to participate in the work of drafting the initial treaties. However, Harold Macmillan, the Foreign Secretary, had responded very coldly. In the event, only an Under-Secretary from the Board of Trade was sent to represent Britain on the Spaak Committee.

Moreover, the differences between Britain and the Six, especially over tariffs became clear very quickly.[6] The British representative, therefore, was withdrawn from the Spaak Committee.[7]

It was not until the beginning of 1956 that Britain, under US pressure, turned her attention again to Europe and proposed the idea of a European free trade area which would include the Six, Great Britain and the other OEEC countries. The British themselves had no real enthusiasm for this idea — Commonwealth trade was still considered to be of much greater importance than European trade — but the idea had been pushed by other OEEC members. Britain, in search of some solution, had reluctantly taken up the idea. After a detailed study had been prepared by the OEEC, in October 1956 Eden presented a British plan for a free trade area in all goods except foodstuffs. This plan did in fact mark a considerable step forward in British thinking and attracted some support in Europe. Both Ludwig Erhardt in Germany and Pierre Mendes-France in France were impressed, for it offered the prospect not only of an enlarged trading market for industrialists, but it also tied Britain more securely to Europe. And in retrospect a good case can be made out to the effect that Europe made a mistake in rejecting it. But rejected it was and there were a number of sound economic reasons for this.[8] Britain never paid sufficient attention to these French objections. Instead, she assumed too readily that Europe would do almost anything to entice her in. Britain totally misgauged the strength of pro-common market sentiment. The Rome Treaties therefore were signed without her. It was a great divide in the history of modern Europe. Britain, excluded from the Common Market, eventually established the European Free Trade Association (EFTA) consisting of the Scandinavian countries, Austria, Portugal and Switzerland. This was established by the Stockholm Convention of 4 January 1960 which, unlike the Common Market Treaty, contained no supra-nationalist element. Nor did the free trade area apply to agricultural products. Thus, by 1960 it was clear that Western Europe was economically divided.

The First British Application

The British seemed little disturbed by these developments. As one recent study of Britain stated:

12

The First British Application

Few people in Britain at the time, however, took much notice of these developments. Britain was still regarded by the British as the leading power in Europe and there was little expectation even in official circles that the Common Market would amount to very much. The Liberal Party argued for British entry but its voice carried little political weight.[9]

This position was to be dramatically changed, however, by the decision of the Macmillan government to seek membership of the EEC. Britain's historic decision to apply to join the EEC was taken slowly. In many respects the application was far from honest. For the real motives behind the application had not been the same as those of the European federalists. Macmillan certainly had no intention of making Britain a 'European power'. The real reason behind the British application was the need to find a theatre in which Britain could act the leading role and thereby increase her reputation on the international stage. Once inside the Common Market, Macmillan planned to organise it into a sort of 'second pillar' of western defence and lead it, in cooperation with America, as part of an extended Atlantic partnership.[10] Thus Britain's decision to apply for membership of the Community did not constitute a new departure but should be seen rather as a means of restoring Britain to her old position at the intersection of the three circles — Europe, America and the Commonwealth. Thus when Macmillan announced Britain's decision to join the Common Market in July 1961 it was stated bluntly that a disruption of 'long-standing and historic ties' with the Commonwealth would be a major loss. The political implications were almost entirely discounted and the Prime Minister spoke of the application as a 'purely economic and trading negotiation'.

Political reaction to Britain's application was rather muted. Little was known in the country about the Common Market and it attracted relatively little interest. Macmillan's matter-of-fact announcement in the Commons was greeted, therefore, with indifference by MPs. The reaction from the Labour Front Brench, however, demonstrated that if Macmillan should change his tune over federalism, Labour was ready to move into action. Gaitskell maintained that public opinion was not yet ripe for European federalism and warned that Britain should not neglect her Commonwealth ties. It was only gradually that the Labour Party united in opposition to entering Europe.[11]

The probability had always been that the Labour Party

would oppose a British application. The Shadow Cabinet was strongly against entry, reflecting the views of a majority of the parliamentary party. Thus although such leading figures as George Brown and Ray Gunter were committed pro-Marketeers, they were unable to make their views prevail against the doubts of colleagues such as Barbara Castle, Richard Crossman, Denis Healey and James Callaghan. Significantly, the party's spokesman on foreign affairs, Harold Wilson, was also unenthusiastic about the Market and his speeches on the subject at this time were hostile to British entry.

Most important of all, it was the clearly and passionately enunciated opposition of Gaitskell himself in his speech to the party conference which finally swung Labour towards an expressly hostile position. Entry into the Common Market declared Gaitskell, would mean 'the end of a thousand years of British history'. The Labour Party agreed and hence the party was now firmly opposed to Macmillan's initiative.

Both inside the country as a whole and inside the Labour Party in particular, opposition had been mounting, partly as a result of the difficulties experienced by the government in securing Commonwealth support for the British application. Thus further pressure was exerted on the British negotiating team, led by Edward Heath, to do more to safeguard Commonwealth interests.

Heath was a late convert to the cause of Europe. He was first given office by Macmillan after 1959, rising to become Lord Privy Seal with special responsibility for European affairs. He was a natural candidate to be put in charge of the negotiations in Brussels and his opening statement to the Commission (made in Paris in October 1961) seemed to start the negotiations well. At the same time his task was necessarily one of safeguarding the interests of Great Britain and the Commonwealth — not to mention her EFTA partners. Hence he could expect to meet with stiff resistance once negotiations got under way in earnest. However, negotiations could not get seriously under way until the Six had first of all settled important problems of their own — in particular the mechanics involved in the adoption of a Common Agricultural Policy.[12] Negotiations between the Six on this complicated subject took a long time to complete, with eventual agreement not being reached until January 1962. The main beneficiary of the new system was France, who had made it clear that she would only countenance industrial competition from Germany and Britain if her agricultural base was protected first. It clearly also followed that France was in no mood to make concessions of any sort to Britain over agricultural imports from the Commonwealth. Negotiations at last got under way in the spring of 1962 and some progress was made on other Commonwealth problems before negotiations were adjourned on 5 August. At this stage there was still optimism over a possible deal. Negotiations were resumed in October but once again it was the problem of British agriculture which proved the most difficult stumbling block. Britain's request for a long transition period in order to change over from her traditional system of farming subsidies, low food prices and cheap Commonwealth food to the Common Agricultural Policy of high prices and levies on imported food was not acceptable to the Commission. The EEC naturally demanded that Britain should apply the Common Policy from the time she entered the Market. Deadlock seemed inevitable. The British negotiators clearly understood that Parliament — not to mention British public opinion — would never agree to such impossible demands.

Macmillan, meanwhile, had been trying to win over the French in another way, by attempting to demonstrate to General de Gaulle that Britain and France could cooperate in Europe on certain political issues. Macmillan went out of his way to let it be known that he agreed with de Gaulle, that Europe should be organised on the basis of a *'Europe des états'* or a *'Europe des nations'* rather than through supra-national political institutions. But his plans to effect some sort of entente with the French President were destined to ultimate failure. There was an ironic conclusion to Macmillan's manoeuvring when de Gaulle suspected agreement was being sought at his expense. Macmillan's other political initiatives with America and West Germany had meanwhile also failed.[13] Thus it proved impossible to resolve the economic divisions between Britain and France by recourse to diplomatic bargaining. On 14 January 1963, at a time when Heath was set to propose a package deal to the Commission, the British application was vetoed by de Gaulle. De Gaulle's veto not only marked the end of hopes of expanding the EEC, it also destroyed Macmillan's foreign policy. At the same time the mood in Britain was one of disinterest and disillusion in the Common Market. The British, in particular, refused to see de Gaulle's veto as a national defeat or humiliation. It was an irrational and selfish act such as might be expected of the French. The experience of negotiating with the Common Market had so disillusioned even the British who had taken an interest in it that the final blow of the General's veto had been accepted with a sigh of relief. People simply wondered why there had been all the fuss in the first place and the serious setback which had been received by the government was therefore only dimly understood.

The Second Try

No further application to join the EEC was made by Britain until May 1967. By this time, much had happened, not least in British domestic politics. The thirteen years of Conservative Government had ended in October 1964 when Harold Wilson, Gaitskell's successor as Leader of the Labour Party, won a narrow electoral victory over Sir Alec Douglas-Home. After less than two years in office with a dangerously thin majority, Wilson went to the polls in 1966 and secured a comfortable election victory.

The fact that Britain's second application to join the EEC came from a Labour Government was itself somewhat surprising.[14] Historically, as we have seen, Labour had never shown any fervour for the cause of the EEC. During the early 1960s most Labour leaders had shown a consistent lack of enthusiasm for the European Community and little real interest or appreciation of the benefits that might accrue for Britain. Labour's attitude during Heath's 1961-63 negotiations had been reflected in Gaitskell's hostile speech at the 1962 Labour Party Conference. During the 1966 election, in a major speech at Bristol, Wilson's position differed very little from Gaitskell's earlier declaration. In this speech, Wilson reiterated the two main Gaitskellite conditions: namely full British independence in respect of foreign and defence policies, and freedom for Britain to continue to buy its food without hindrance in world markets. Wilson, however, restated that his own position remained as it always had been: a commitment to entry if the terms were right.

In office, however, Wilson slowly began to change his views. He was increasingly aware of the degree to which Britain's power and influence in the world had diminished. It was also equally apparent to Wilson that the Commonwealth was clearly not the instrument it had been in the early 1960s. In addition, the problems of defending sterling and also the French withdrawal from NATO all inclined Wilson to look towards Europe. Even so, Wilson moved over only slowly towards full conversion. In May 1965, at an EFTA Conference in Vienna, the possibility of forming closer links between EFTA and the EEC had been discussed. Even when this was seen to be unrealistic, Wilson toyed with *association* with the EEC under Article 238 of the Treaty of Rome rather than commit himself to a full-scale application.

Gradually, Wilson saw there was no alternative to EEC entry. But Wilson also knew that he would face a tough battle with his Cabinet and the Party. Within the Cabinet, the strongest supporters of entry were George Brown (although Crossman's diaries suggest Brown had some private doubts), and Roy Jenkins. Crosland also was enthusiastic, while Michael Stewart, the Foreign Secretary, was now also in favour. Wilson may also have been influenced by wider evidence of support — the recently-formed Confederation of British Industry was enthusiastic for Europe and an opinion poll in July 1966 showed 75% favouring entry. In Europe itself, Italy and the Benelux countries were keen on British entry and would put their influence behind Britain.

A highly important Cabinet meeting on 22 October 1966 marked an important stage in the Government's path. The Cabinet had before it the report of the Committee, chaired by George Brown, on the social and economic implications of joining. This report greatly strengthened the case for entry and Wilson appears to have been strongly influenced by it. Although the Cabinet remained divided, it agreed that Wilson and Brown should tour the capitals of the EEC countries early in 1967. On 10 November 1966 Wilson announced in the House of Commons that the question of British entry into the European Community would be explored anew.

The tour of Continental capitals was duly undertaken by Wilson and George Brown, during the early months of 1967. These soundings convinced Wilson to apply, even though there had been warnings from the Paris Embassy of the possibility of another veto by de Gaulle.

In due course, after an historic Cabinet meeting on 2 May

17

1967, Wilson announced the Labour Government's intention to apply for full membership of the European Community. There were no resignations from Wilson's Cabinet when the decision was made, although there was evidence that seven of the 21 ministers were hostile, ten were in favour and six, according to Crossman, were 'possible' supporters. Not surprisingly, the Conservative opposition welcomed Wilson's move. Although, earlier, some 107 Labour MPs had tabled a motion on 21 February recalling their party's stiff conditions for entry, Wilson's powerful support of the pro-Market case at a series of party meetings won a clear majority of the Parliamentary Labour Party into a pro-EEC position. In October, both the National Executive Committee and the Party Conference gave Wilson substantial backing.

Partly, Wilson's success could be explained by the fact that the natural leaders of the anti-EEC movement were in the Cabinet. The anti-marketeers had to rely on such veterans as Manny Shinwell to lead their cause. Nonetheless, despite Wilson's powers of persuasion, there was a strong contingent of Labour MPs still hostile. Some 74 Labour MPs signed the Tribune anti-market manifesto. On 10 May the House of Commons supported the government with an overwhelming majority — 488 votes to 62, but thirty-five Labour MPs voted against entry and some fifty abstained.

Wilson's EEC initiative on Europe came to a sudden end. On 16 May de Gaulle vetoed the British application, announcing that Britain was not yet ready to join the Six. Like Macmillan, Wilson had been baulked in his objective by French opposition and was not able to determine whether or not satisfactory conditions for entry could be obtained. The Labour Government however did not withdraw the British application, but left it on the table.

With the resignation of de Gaulle in April 1969 the political power structure in Europe underwent a major change. At The Hague Summit of December 1969, the six members of the EEC confirmed their desire to complete, strengthen and enlarge the Community. The way was open again for Britain to take her place in Europe. But on this occasion it was to be the Conservative Government of Edward Heath that was finally to achieve the elusive goal of membership of the European Community.

Britain Enters Europe

In the General Election of 18 June 1970, the Conservative Party won a decisive, if unexpected, victory at the polls. During the campaign, all three main parties had fought the election firmly committed to taking Britain into Europe if the terms were right. No one doubted the enthusiasm of Edward Heath for the European cause and the new government moved with speed and vigour to begin negotiations for entry.[15]

The Labour application was immediately 'picked up' by the incoming Conservative Government and negotiations opened in Luxembourg on 30 June. Detailed discussions began in September and ran through to February 1971.

The discussions — though eventually successful — had many hurdles to overcome. France, in particular, was difficult, insisting on an immediate British acceptance of the Common Agricultural Policy (CAP), raising doubts about the sterling balances and attacking the privileged position of the London capital market. By March 1971, there was dismay in the British negotiating team that yet another veto might by imminent — but the vital Heath-Pompidou summit of 20-21 May in Paris resolved many of the difficulties. Britain, this time, could also count on the friendly support of West Germany in the person of Willy Brandt. In the end, the final terms agreed for entry were not over-generous for Britain — although Britain did secure transitional periods of up to six years before the common external tariff, the Common Agricultural Policy and contributions to the Community budget were applied fully. In addition, special transitional terms were agreed for New Zealand, anxious over her dairy products, and the Commonwealth sugar producers.

Negotiating the terms for entry, though crucial, was only the first step for Heath. He had now to carry the legislation through Parliament, with some redoubtable opponents of entry on his own backbenches. At the same time, Labour had become increasingly hostile. Between the de Gaulle veto of 1968 and the application by Heath, opposition in Britain, most particularly in the Labour Party, to EEC entry had hardened. The Common Market Safeguards Campaign had been launched at the end of 1969. Its prominent Labour supporters included Barbara Castle, Ian Mikardo and Peter Shore. The two foremost union leaders — Hugh Scanlon and Jack Jones — were also members,

19

reflecting the growing TUC hostility to entry. Other anti-EEC supporters were grouped in the Anti-Common Market League and the Keep Britain Out organisation.

Within a year of their election defeat the Labour Party had swung sharply against Europe — although the leadership continued to emphasise that the terms, not the principle, were the source of their objection.

In a broadcast on 9 July 1971 — replying to one by Heath the previous night, commending the settlement to the nation — Wilson recalled that Labour had set four conditions for membership in 1967. The points on which satisfactory terms must be obtained, Wilson stressed, were the balance of payments, the effect on sugar, the effect on New Zealand and the scope for control of capital movements that would be left to Britain as an EEC member.

It was on these issues that the Tory terms should be judged. A special conference called by the Labour Party to debate the issue, which took place in London on 17 July, was largely hostile. George Thomson, a prominent Marketeer who had been one of the Ministerial negotiators, said he would have recommended a Labour cabinet to accept the terms the Conservative Government had obtained. No vote was taken on the issue. Two days later the deputy leader, Roy Jenkins, told the Parliamentary Party he believed a Labour government would have accepted the terms. But on 28 July the Party's National Executive passed a resolution condemning them. Labour conference voted against entry by a substantial majority in October; the Conservative and Liberal conferences produced substantial majorities in favour.

The Commons debated the application from 21 to 28 October, 1971. There was a free vote on the Conservative side, a course which, the Conservative business managers correctly calculated, would encourage Labour's Marketeers to defy their own anti-Market whip and thus more than cancel out the expected defections on the Conservative side.

The European Communities Bill, the Bill which effectively took Britain into Europe, turned out to be unexpectedly short; it had only 12 clauses and four schedules of which the most crucial was Clause II, which allowed Westminster legislation to be over-ridden by legislation from Brussels. Labour and Conservative anti-Marketeers argued that this represented an

unacceptable surrender of the sovereignty of Parliament. One
Conservative, Enoch Powell, regarded this matter as of such
supreme importance that he later counselled the Conservatives
to vote for the Labour Party in the 1974 General Election, and
did so himself. But government spokesmen said this surrender
of sovereignty was implicit in any move to join Europe and
would certainly have been accepted by Labour had they got in
in 1967.
The Bill took five months to complete its progress through
the Commons. There were 104 divisions. The lowest majority,
on a vote on the free movement of capital, was four. The
crucial second reading, on 17 February, was approved by 309
votes to 301, a majority of eight.
The most severe divisions in the Labour Party over the Bill
occurred in April, when the Shadow Cabinet decided to support
an amendment tabled by a prominent Conservative anti-
Marketeer, Neil Marten, calling for a consultative referendum
before a final decision on entry. Until then, Labour had been
opposed to a referendum. The Shadow Cabinet decision pre-
cipitated the resignation of the deputy leader of the party,
Roy Jenkins.
The referendum proposal was defeated by 284 votes to 235,
a Government majority of 49, with 63 Labour MPs abstaining.
The Bill then went on to pass its third reading on 13 July by
301 to 284, a majority of 17 and Britain entered the Community on 1 January 1973. At the third attempt, and with the
nation still deeply divided over the question of membership,
Britain had belatedly taken her place in Europe.

The 1975 Referendum

The entry of Britain into the Community on 1 January 1973
failed to end the bitter debate in the country over the merits of
membership. Once again, it was developments in domestic
politics which brought the European issue back into the fore-
front of the political arena. In February 1974, against a background of almost unprecedented industrial militancy and with
the country in the throes of a three-day week, the Heath
Government called a general election. Its gamble to secure a
new mandate failed. Wilson became Prime Minister and,
after the shortest Parliament of modern times, called an election for October 1974. During these months, hostility to the

Common Market within many sections of the Labour movement remained as implacable as ever. Hence, the Labour Party's
manifesto for the October election had promised that within a
year the people would decide 'through the ballot box' whether
Britain should stay in the European Common Market on the
terms to be renegotiated by the Labour Government, or reject
them and leave the Community. This formula left the option
open between a referendum and yet another election in 1975.
On 22 January 1975 the Government announced that they
would bring in a Referendum Bill. The White Paper published
on 26 February established that there would be a national
count. The decision was to be by a simple majority on the
question 'Do you think the UK should stay in the European
Community?' In the debate on the White Paper, the principle
of this direct consultation of the electors, a hitherto unknown
British constitutional practice, was approved in the House of
Commons by 312 votes to 262, five Conservatives voting with
the Government and one Labour MP with the Opposition. The
Government's original intention for a single national declaration
was lost during the debate. On a free vote on 23 April it was
decided by 270 votes to 153, against strong Government
pressure, that the result should be declared regionally: a Liberal
motion for declaration by constituencies was lost by 264 votes
to 131.

On 18 March Wilson informed the Commons that the
Government had decided to recommend a Yes vote. The
Cabinet, however, was split 16 to 7. The 'No' faction numbered
Michael Foot (Secretary of State for Employment), Tony Benn
(Industry), Peter Shore (Trade), Barbara Castle (Social Services),
Eric Varley (Energy), William Ross (Scotland), and John Silkin
(Planning and Local Government). It was an extraordinary state
of affairs. Should the rebel Ministers resign? Wilson neatly resolved the problem by stating that, while dissident Ministers
would otherwise be free to express themselves as they wished, all
Ministers speaking from the despatch box would reflect Government policy. Apart from the dismissal of Eric Heffer, the Minister
of State for Industry, this extraordinary Cabinet agreement to
differ on a vital issue operated without resignations right through
the referendum.

Though the Cabinet remained intact, the deep divisions
within the Labour ranks remained as wide as ever. On 19 March

a resolution signed by 18 out of 29 members of the National Executive recommended to a special party conference, successfully demanded by the left wing, that the party should campaign for withdrawal from the EEC. Later, in the Commons vote on the Government's pro-Market White Paper, 145 Labour MPs went into the No lobby, against 138 Ayes and 32 abstentions. The special conference on 26 April voted two to one for withdrawal.

Following the EEC summit meeting in Dublin on 10 and 11 March, when the assembled heads of government ratified certain decisions favourable to Britain which were regarded as part of the renegotiations, the Government's White Paper, *Membership of the EEC: Report on Renegotiation* was published on 27 March. After describing the better terms which the Government claimed it had won, it concluded: 'Continued membership of the Community is in Britain's interest . . . In the Government's view the consequences of withdrawal would be adverse.'

The White Paper went on to consider general questions such as sovereignty, the European Parliament, Community legislation, the value of membership for Britain's world role, and the effects of withdrawal, which, it said, would threaten the political stability of Western Europe.

In the House of Commons on 9 April the White Paper was endorsed by a margin of 226 votes (393 to 170), more than double the majority of 112 recorded in October 1971 for the principle of entering the EEC. In many respects, the claims and counter-claims of the debate had all been heard before. The 'Yes' side had a clear propaganda advantage in the support of most business firms, who did not hesitate to use their money, their advertising power and their communications with their workers, and of the great majority of the national and regional press. The contest cut right across party lines. Politicians as far apart as Enoch Powell and Michael Foot united in the 'No' lobby.

The 'Yes' lobby included such unusual allies as the majority of the Labour Cabinet, the bulk of the Tory and Liberal parties, the Confederation of British Industry, the National Farmers Union and the City of London. Three pamphlets were duly delivered to every household in the kingdom. One was the Government's 'popular version of the White Paper'. The others, each half the size, were produced by the umbrella organisations 'Britain in Europe' and 'The National Referendum Campaign', and were straightforward exercises in public relations. The outcome fulfilled the best hopes of the pro-Marketeers. Turnout was high and the majority for Yes was over two to one. The figures were: Yes 17,378,581 (67.2%), No 8,470,073 (32.8%). England voted 68.7% Yes, Wales 65.6%, Scotland 54.4% and Ulster 52.1%. Not only every one of the four national segments of the United Kingdom but also every English and Welsh region voted Yes. The only two No majorities anywhere were recorded in two sparsely populated northern areas, the Shetlands and the Western Isles. The full details are set out in Table 1.

The outcome was a triumph for the ardent champions of Britain in Europe — most particularly Edward Heath. But it was also a triumph for the astute political tactics of Harold Wilson. The left of his party had been appeased by the holding of the referendum, the right by its result. The Wilson-Callaghan combination, having at last come down on the Yes side, and been backed by the electorate, gained prestige as a national leadership. Other consequences also followed the 'Yes' vote. Labour belatedly sent a team to the European Parliament, and British trade unionists joined their appropriate European organisations. Labour had survived intact the Common Market issue. The arguments over the continuation of British membership — if not totally buried — had been decisively and very probably irreversibly settled. But this did not mean that divisions over European policy were stilled. Over such issues as European Monetary Union old passions were renewed. And the coming of Direct Elections (see pp. 56-74) witnessed a renewal of old political divisions.

The 1975 Referendum

TABLE 1   THE 1975 REFERENDUM*

The voting nationally was as follows:

'Yes' votes	17,378,581	67.2%
'No' votes	8,470,073	32.8%
'Yes' majority	8,908,508	

	Yes	%	No	%	% Poll
ENGLAND					
Avon	310,145	67.8	147,024	32.2	68.7
Bedfordshire	154,338	69.4	67,969	30.6	67.9
Berkshire	215,184	72.6	81,221	27.4	66.4
Buckinghamshire	180,512	74.3	62,578	25.7	69.5
Cambridgeshire	177,789	74.1	62,143	25.9	62.9
Cheshire	290,714	70.1	123,839	29.9	65.5
Cleveland	158,982	67.3	77,079	32.7	60.2
Cornwall	137,828	68.5	63,478	31.5	66.8
Cumbria	162,545	71.9	63,564	28.1	64.8
Derbyshire	286,614	68.6	131,457	31.4	64.1
Devon	334,244	72.1	129,179	27.9	68.0
Dorset	217,432	73.3	78,239	26.5	68.3
Durham	175,284	64.2	97,724	35.8	61.5
Essex	463,505	67.7	222,085	32.4	67.7
Gloucestershire	170,931	71.7	67,465	28.3	68.4
Gr. London	2,201,031	66.7	1,100,185	33.3	60.8
Gr. Manchester	797,316	64.5	439,191	35.5	64.1
Hampshire	484,302	71.0	197,761	29.0	68.0
Hereford and Worcs.	203,128	72.8	75,779	27.2	66.4
Hertfordshire	326,943	70.4	137,226	29.6	70.2
Humberside	257,826	67.8	122,199	32.2	62.4
Isle of Wight	40,837	71.2	17,375	29.8	67.5
Isles of Scilly	802	74.5	275	25.5	75.0
Kent	493,407	70.4	207,358	29.6	67.4
Lancashire	455,170	68.6	208,821	31.4	67.2
Leicestershire	291,500	73.3	106,004	26.7	66.4
Lincolnshire	180,603	74.7	61,011	25.3	63.7
Merseyside	465,625	64.8	252,712	35.2	62.7
Norfolk	218,883	70.1	93,198	29.9	63.8

* Source: John Paxton, *Dictionary of the EEC*, pp. 213-215.

25

TABLE 1 — *cont.*

	Yes	%	No	%	% Poll
Northamptonshire	162,803	69.5	71,322	30.5	65.0
Northumberland	95,980	69.2	42,645	30.8	65.0
Nottinghamshire	297,191	66.8	147,461	33.2	67.7
Oxfordshire	179,938	73.6	64,643	26.4	67.7
Salop	113,044	72.3	43,329	27.7	62.0
Somerset	138,830	69.6	60,631	30.4	67.7
Staffordshire	306,518	67.4	148,252	32.6	64.3
Suffolk	187,484	72.2	72,251	27.8	64.9
Surrey	386,369	76.2	120,576	23.8	70.1
East Sussex	249,780	74.3	86,198	25.7	68.6
West Sussex	242,890	76.2	73,928	23.8	68.6
Tyne and Wear	344,069	62.9	202,511	37.1	62.7
Warwickshire	156,303	69.9	67,221	30.1	68.0
West Midlands	801,913	65.1	429,207	34.9	62.5
Wiltshire	172,791	71.7	68,113	28.3	67.8
North Yorkshire	234,040	76.3	72,805	23.7	64.3
South Yorkshire	377,916	63.4	217,792	36.6	62.4
West Yorkshire	616,730	65.4	326,993	34.6	63.6
WALES					
Clwyd	123,980	69.1	55,424	30.9	65.8
Dyfed	109,184	67.6	52,264	32.4	67.5
Mid Glamorgan	147,348	56.9	111,672	43.1	66.6
South Glamorgan	127,932	69.5	56,224	30.5	66.7
West Glamorgan	112,989	61.6	70,316	38.4	67.4
Gwent	132,557	62.1	80,992	37.9	68.2
Gwynedd	76,421	70.6	31,807	29.4	64.3
Powys	38,724	74.3	13,372	25.7	67.9
SCOTLAND					
Borders	34,092	72.3	13,053	27.7	63.2
Central	71,986	59.7	48,568	40.3	64.1
Dumfries and Galloway	42,608	68.2	19,856	31.8	61.5
Fife	84,239	56.3	65,260	43.7	63.3
Grampian	108,520	58.2	78,071	41.8	57.4
Highland	40,802	54.6	33,979	45.4	58.7
Lothian	208,133	59.5	141,456	40.5	63.6
Orkney	3,911	61.8	2,419	38.2	48.2
Shetland*	2,815	43.7	3,631	56.3	47.1
Strathclyde	625,939	57.7	459,073	42.3	61.7
Tayside	105,728	58.6	74,567	41.4	63.8
Western Isles*	3,393	29.5	8,106	70.5	50.1
NORTHERN IRELAND					
Northern Ireland	259,251	52.1	237,911	47.9	47.4

* Returned majority votes against EEC membership.

Footnotes

1. For a fuller discussion of this period see W.O. Henderson, *The Genesis of the Common Market* (London, 1962).
2. Alan Sked, *Post-War Britain: A Political History* (London, 1979).
3. Sked, *op. cit.*
4. *Ibid.*
5. Among the most useful books on this period is John Paxton, *The Developing Common Market* (London, 1976).
6. In particular they held different views regarding the proposed external tariff. The Six supported the view they they should establish a single tariff structure with regard to the rest of the world, thus strengthening their hand in tariff negotiations. Britain on the other hand, would not accept the idea of a common external tariff. She had her system of Commonwealth preferences to protect; she wanted to retain the OEEC as the European organisation responsible for conducting tariff-negotiations; and she disliked the supra-national implications of a Common Market external tariff.
7. Eden, who was absorbed with problems in the Middle East and with relations with the Soviet Union, probably placed little significance on what was happening.
8. The French, for example, were clearly scared at the prospect of being subjected to both British and German industrial competition while securing no advantage for their farm products. Furthermore, if there were no common external tariff on agricultural imports a country like Britain which had access to cheap food from her Commonwealth might well be able to cut costs on her wage bill and hence be able to under-cut her European industrial competitors.
9. See Alan Sked, *op. cit.*
10. Thus it was significant that the Prime Minister had, therefore, taken pains to secure United States approval for his plans, approval which Kennedy was only too eager to give. He, too, regretted Europe's division into two western camps (EEC and EFTA) and looked to European trade and economic union to lay the foundation for a really strong NATO.
11. For Labour's attitude, see D. Butler, *The British General Election of 1959* (London, 1960).
12. These were to consist of a system of levies on agricultural imports, a system of supports for European agriculture (maintained through a Common Agricultural Fund), and a system of subsidies for European agricultural exports.
13. He had tried to encourage the Americans to allow him to pass on nuclear knowledge to France and to persuade Chancellor Adenauer to give him the special support of West Germany. In the first case, the Americans would not agree while in the second, Adenauer, who had never got over the allied refusal to demolish the Berlin Wall (erected in 1961) and who did not trust Macmillan in any case (he considered the Prime Minister too ready to deal with the Russians) would not endanger his special relationship with France to help the

The Background to British Entry into Europe

British out.

14. For a detailed discussion see U. Kitzinger, *Diplomacy and Persuasion* (London, 1973).
15. For the successful Conservative application see D. Butler and D. Kavanagh, *The British General Election of February 1974* (London, 1974).
16. On the referendum, see D. Butler and U. Kitzinger, *The 1975 Referendum* (London, 1976).

28

Chapter 2

The European Community

Introduction

Despite the protracted debate over Britain's entry into the EEC, many of the main institutions and organisations of the Community have remained a mystery to many British voters. This chapter sets out, in alphabetical order, the key names and phrases which have become the core of the political vocabulary of the EEC.

Accession, Treaty of. This treaty was signed in Brussels on 22 January 1972, so it is sometimes known as the Treaty of Brussels. It set out the terms under which Denmark, Ireland, Norway and the United Kingdom should join Belgium, France, the Federal Republic of Germany, Italy, Luxembourg and the Netherlands in the European Economic Community, Euratom and the European Coal and Steel Community. The Treaty enlarged the Community institutions to accommodate the new members, and provided for a transitional period before they were obliged fully to adopt existing policies. Following a referendum decision not to join the Community Norway did not ratify the Treaty. Denmark, Ireland and the United Kingdom became members of the Community on 1 January 1973.

Accords of Luxembourg. In 1965 France, under the presidency of General de Gaulle, withdrew from most of the activities of the European Community. This dispute was resolved in January 1966 on the basis of statements known as the Accords of Luxembourg. The dispute was caused by a set of proposals for financing the EEC Common Agricultural Policy which involved giving the EEC resources in its own right and extending the control of European Parliament over them. Underlying

29

the problems was de Gaulle's opposition to any increase in the powers of the Community institutions or in integration between the member states. He was anxious that France should retain her freedom of action and resist the influence within Europe of the USA.

France disliked the way in which the Commission of the EEC had been coming to be seen as an institution on a par with the Governments of the member states, and the first part of the Accords dealt with matters such as the control of the operation of Community information services and the reception of foreign ambassadors to the Community. The second part of the Accords recorded a difference of opinion between France and the five other members over the ways in which agreement was reached in the Council of Ministers. The five other members were content to stick to the majority voting arrangements laid down in the Treaties, but France stated that where very important interests were involved decisions should be unanimous. The Accords, while not in this respect constituting an agreement, have usually been taken, for example by the British Government, as allowing each member state a veto over decisions which are regarded as of vital national importance.

Association Agreements with the European Community.
Article 238 of the Treaty of Rome allows the EEC to enter into Association Agreements with non-members covering, for example, the abolition of customs duties on some or all trade between the Associate and the Community. Such agreements, which usually provide for the setting up of joint institutions to supervise the functioning of the Agreement, have been made between the EEC and Greece, Spain, Turkey, Cyprus, and Malta. Trade agreements exist with a number of other countries, such as the former EFTA countries, Egypt, Israel, and Yugoslavia. A large number of African, Caribbean and Pacific states are similarly linked to the European Community through the Lome Convention.

Benelux. In 1944 the governments in exile of Belgium, the Netherlands and Luxembourg signed the Benelux customs convention which from 1948 resulted in a customs union between the three countries. The three were more closely linked by a treaty in 1958 establishing a Benelux economic union. This provided for coordination of economic and social policies and for the free movement of people, goods, capital and services between the three countries. These arrangements have since been overshadowed by the general development of the European Community as a whole within which the Benelux countries originally formed a more closely-linked group.

Budget of the European Communities. The European Community has to pay for the administrative expenses of its institutions, and the costs of its policies, for example, the Regional policy, financed through the Regional Development Fund, the Social policy, through the Social Fund, and the Common Agricultural Policy, which alone accounts for some two-thirds of Community expenditure. The Treaties establishing the European Coal and Steel Community, Euratom and the European Economic Community have laid down procedures for establishing and handling a Budget for this expenditure. These arrangements were consolidated and amended by treaties signed in April 1970 and July 1975. The effect of these treaties has been to increase the powers of the European Parliament in relation to the Budget. An initial Budget is drawn up by the Commission and discussed and amended by the Council of Ministers. It is then passed to the Parliament which has the right to oppose modifications to expenditure arising directly from the Treaties (obligatory expenditure), which may however, be over-ruled by the Council of Ministers. Other expenditure (non-obligatory expenditure) may be subject to amendments by the Parliament. A 'concertation' mechanism, first used over the Regional Development Fund in 1975, exists to resolve disputes between the Parliament and the Council of Ministers, for example over the division of expenditure between the two categories. The European Parliament may reject the Budget in its entirety, obliging the Commission to present a new one. In 1977 the Budget, in total, amounted to the equivalent of approximately one-fifth of the United Kingdom's public expenditure that year.

Commission of the European Communities. The Commission consists of thirteen members, two each from France, Italy, West Germany and the United Kingdom, and one each from Belgium, Denmark, Luxembourg and Ireland. They are appointed, by agreement between the governments of the member states, for four-year terms, and one of them is chosen as President for a two year period, which can be renewed. They form an independent, collective body, and although each has responsibility for particular aspects of the Community they take their decisions jointly. Their independence is ensured by the provision that they can only be dismissed as a body, and only by a vote of the European Parliament. The Commission's most important function is to formulate Community policy. The Council of Ministers may make decisions upon Community legislation only on the basis of proposals from the Commission. It is also responsible for ensuring that member states abide by their Treaty undertakings, and may bring them before the Court of Justice should they fail to do so. The Commission acts as negotiator on behalf of the Community in international negotiations involving Community policy. The Commission has some executive powers and may make some regulations covering the detailed application of Community policies. The Commission, whose main offices are in the Berlaymont Building in Brussels, employed over 8,600 administrative staff in 1978, of whom one in eight was a language specialist (translators, interpreters). The staff are divided into Directorates-General, each concerned with a particular field of the Community's activities.

Committee of Permanent Representatives (COREPER). Each member state is represented in Brussels by a Permanent Representative, with the rank of Ambassador. These representatives, who are senior national officials, form a committee, which meets on a regular weekly basis. There is also a regular meeting of their deputies, and business is divided between the two groups on the basis of its subject matter. There is a parallel committee, the Special Committee on Agriculture, for agricultural matters. The Committee acts on behalf of the member states in examining proposals for legislation and for policy (for example, for the Community's position in international negotiations) produced by the Commission. These proposals will usually have been subject to preliminary consideration in working groups of national officials; the Committee of Permanent Representatives attempts to resolve any outstanding difficulties. If they can do so, the proposed legislation or policy can be endorsed by the Council of Ministers without further discussion, if not the issues are further debated by the next meeting of the Council of Ministers concerned with the appropriate topic. A representative of the Commission is present at the meetings of the Committee, but the Committee's proceedings, being essentially inter-governmental negotiations, are confidential.

Common Agricultural Policy. This controversial policy is based upon two principles, price support and domestic protection. In the uncertain conditions of world agricultural markets these principles may act to ensure stability of supply and reasonable prices; at the same time they have not been able to prevent the accumulation of surpluses (butter mountains and wine lakes) and prices which are well above those on world markets. Article 39 of the Treaty of Rome sets out the objectives of a Community agricultural policy as

1) to increase agricultural productivity
2) to ensure a fair standard of living for the agricultural population
3) to stabilise markets
4) to guarantee supplies
5) to ensure reasonable prices to consumers.

The first principle means that the farmer is supported directly by the consumer (and not, for example, by subsidies provided from the general taxation of the whole population) through the fixing of prices that will ensure him a reasonable income. If he cannot sell his goods at this price the Community, through its national intervention agencies, will buy them. The second principle protects the farmer against competition from imports by taxing them so as to bring their prices up to Community levels. The Common Agricultural Policy is also intended to improve the structure of agriculture through the provision of up-to-date equipment and the amalgamation of small farms, though this aspect of the policy has not had the same importance as the pricing and marketing policies and national measures still have a major part to play. Problems have arisen as the result of changes in the exchange values of national currencies; because these changes were reflected in the income of the farmers when the prices were calculated in the original Community unit of account a special unit of account, 'green currency' such as the 'green pound', is now used. The Common Agricultural Policy is managed by management committees for each commodity, composed of national representatives, whose decisions may be over-ruled by the Commission, which also has powers to make many of the detailed regulations. Should there be a continued dispute the Council of Ministers has the final voice. The policy is financed by the Agricultural Guidance and Guarantee Fund, provided for under the Community Budget.

Common Market. This phrase, often used to refer to the European Economic Community, in fact describes only one aspect of the Community. Article 2 of the Treaty of Rome says that the creation of a common market is one of the main means for the achievement of the aims of the Treaty signatories. A common market involves the abolition of customs duties between members, the establishment of a common tariff on imports, the abolition of barriers to trade between members, free movement of capital and labour between them, and certain common policies.

Consultative Committee of the European Coal and Steel Community. This Committee consists of eighty-one members appointed by the Council of Ministers, plus one observer. The members, who serve in a personal capacity, are chosen from producers, workers, consumers and dealers in the coal, steel, iron-ore and scrap industries. It must, under the Treaty, be consulted on certain measures taken by the Coal and Steel Community, and its opinion is sought on all important questions concerning the Community's policies and functioning. This Committee is the equivalent, for the Coal and Steel Community, of the Economic and Social Committee of the EEC and Euratom.

Council of Ministers. The Council of Ministers has the final voice in making European Community policy and enacting European Community law. The regulations which it may issue are law, as direct and binding within each member state as the laws passed by the state's own legislature. The Council consists of one ministerial representative from each member state, but its composition varies depending on the subject under discussion, thus an agriculture council is attended by Ministers of

Agriculture, a transport council by Ministers of Transport. The Council of Foreign Ministers is regarded as being the senior body, and the Foreign Minister of the country holding the chairmanship (presidency) of the Council for the time being is regarded as the President of the Council. The member states take it in turns, by alphabetical order, to hold the chairmanship for six months. The Council meets in Luxembourg in April, June and October, and in Brussels at other times. The Council may not itself initiate policy of legislation. It must take decisions on the basis of proposals from the Commission, although it may ask the Commission to submit certain proposals. According to the Treaties, decisions may be arrived at by a system of weighted majority voting. However, agreement is more usually reached through negotiations, packages and compromises, and may involve lengthy 'marathon' sessions. Some member states insist upon a right of veto where they consider vital national interests are at stake. The Council is supported by a secretariat of about 1,200 staff, based largely in the Charlemagne building in Brussels. It is also supported by an extensive network of inter-governmental working groups, consisting of national officials, with COREPER at their apex, which consider both legislation and policy. The members of the Council of Ministers represent their own governments and countries, and are not obliged to take any 'community interest' into account, though the members of the Commission, present at the meetings, try to ensure that a 'Community' decision is reached. The Council of Ministers considers the opinions of the Economic and Social Committee and of the European Parliament, but is not obliged to heed them. It is not responsible to the European Parliament, which does, however, have the right to put questions to the Council. Replies have to be agreed between the member states and are delivered by the presidency for the time being.

Court of Justice of the European Community. This Court, which sits in Luxembourg, consists of nine judges, who sit together on all cases and make decisions by majority vote. Dissenting judgments are not published. The judges are assisted by four advocates-general, who give a summing up and expert legal opinion at the end of each case. The Court is the final arbiter for all legal questions concerning the EEC, the European

Coal and Steel Community and Euratom. The Court hears disputes under the treaties between member states and between member states and the Community institutions. It also hears cases where individuals of firms directly affected wish to challenge the legality of a Community action. It may hear appeals from member states, the Commission or the Council of Ministers. The main work of enforcing Community law falls on the national courts of each country, for Community law operates within each state as if it were national legislation. However, national courts may refer questions of interpretation to the European Court of Justice for a ruling.

Directives of the European Community. Directives are, with Regulations and Decisions, one of the forms which legislation made under the Treaty of Rome and the Euratom Treaty may take. The corresponding form of legislation under the Coal and Steel Community Treaty (the Treaty of Paris) is called a Recommendation. Directives are made by the Council of Ministers on the basis of proposals from the Commission. They are addressed to the governments of member states and are binding on them as to the results to be achieved, but leave open the method by which these results are to be obtained. Often they are implemented by legislation made by the member states' national legislatures.

Economic and Monetary Union within the European Community. By the late 1960s the development of the EEC and the emergence of some common policies, especially the Common Agricultural Policy, focused attention on the problems that could be caused by the lack of a common economic and monetary policy and particularly by matters such as fluctuating exchange rates between member states. The first Barre plan of 1969, approved by the heads of government of the original six members of the Community at the Hague summit in December 1969, the second Barre plan of 1970 and the Werner report of 1970 all set out various proposals for the achievement of economic and monetary union within the Community, with a target date of 1980. However, the effect of the world monetary crisis of the early 1970s, of the oil crisis, and of rapidly rising inflation and unemployment in several member states was to lessen the enthusiasm for economic and monetary union, and bring into prominence some of the difficulties and differences of opinion that it could provoke. Nevertheless, since the early 1970s the mechanisms for consultation between member states on economic and monetary problems have been strengthened, and in 1973 the European Monetary Fund, designed to assist member states in certain economic difficulties was set up. During 1978 it became clear that there was a renewal of interest in the possibility of economic and monetary union within the Community, especially on the part of the French and West German governments.

Economic and Social Committee of the European Community. This is a consultative committee which serves the EEC and Euratom. The corresponding body within the European Coal and Steel Community is the Consultative Committee. The Economic and Social Committee consists of 144 members, 24 each from France, West Germany, Italy and the United Kingdom, 12 each from Belgium and the Netherlands, 9 each from Ireland and Denmark and 6 from Luxembourg. The members are nominated by their national governments, in a personal capacity, and appointed by the Council of Ministers. They are divided into three groups, representing employers, workers, and the general interest (farmers, the professions, and consumer groups, for example). The Commission and the Council of Ministers may, and in come cases must, consult the Committee on proposals, but the Council of Ministers is not obliged to defer to the advice it receives.

Enlargement of the European Community. The European Coal and Steel Community was founded in 1952 between Belgium, France, Italy, Luxembourg, the Netherlands and West Germany. Britain was invited to take part in setting up the ECSC but declined to do so, and also withdrew from the negotiations which led to the setting up of the EEC and Euratom in 1958. In 1961, however, Britain, under Harold Macmillan, applied to open negotiations for membership, which, under the Treaties is open to any European state. Denmark and Ireland, and then Norway, also opened negotiations. In January 1963 the President of France, General de Gaulle, announced that British membership of the Community would be unacceptable, and negotiations with all the applicants were abandoned.

A further application for membership was made by Britain, now under Harold Wilson's Labour government in 1967, and was again turned down by de Gaulle. In December 1969 the original six member states decided that negotiations with Britain, Ireland, Denmark and Norway could be resumed, and Britain, Ireland and Denmark joined in 1973. Following a referendum Norway had failed to ratify the Treaty of Accession.

In 1962 Greece, and in 1974 Turkey, signed association agreements with the Community which envisaged possible developments towards full membership of the Community. With the return to a democratic regime in Greece, negotiations began in 1976 for the transformation of the existing agreement into full membership. While Turkey has indicated that she does not at present wish to take any further steps towards membership, both Spain and Portugal, with the advent of more democratic regimes, have taken steps to apply for full membership. Cyprus and Malta also have association agreements with the Community but no moves have been made to develop them.

Euratom. This is the name by which the European Atomic Energy Community is usually known. It was set up at the same time as the European Economic Community, but by a separate Treaty. The European Parliament, the European Court of Justice, and the Economic and Social Committee have always served both communities, and from 1965 they shared the same Commission and Council of Ministers. Euratom was intended to promote the establishment and growth of nuclear industries, and it was given certain powers to promote research, lay down health and safety standards and establish a common market in nuclear material. Its main activity has in fact proved to be participation in research, especially through the European Community's Joint Research Centre.

European Agricultural Guidance and Guarantee Fund. This is the source of the money used to support farming in the European Community, for example by buying up produce which farmers are otherwise unable to sell at the prices fixed by the Common Agricultural Policy. It was hoped that money required could be provided by, for example, re-selling of the bought-up produce, and levies on imported agricultural goods which were intended to bring their prices up to Community levels. However, the sums required turned out to be far larger than those which accrued from these sources, and most of the money now comes from the Community Budget, approximately two-thirds of which is now spent on the Agricultural Guidance and Guarantee Fund. Just over one-tenth of the Fund's annual expenditure goes towards improving the structure and equipment of European farming.

European Coal and Steel Community. In 1950 Jean Monnet, who had been largely responsible for planning France's postwar recovery and reconstruction, worked out a plan that he hoped would be a first step towards linking the countries of Europe so closely together that war between them would in future be impossible. The important place that the coal and steel industries hold within national economic life, and the position of some coal and iron resources on the borders between France and Germany suggested that the Coal and Steel industries would be a strategic sector with which to start. Jean Monnet put this plan forward to the then French Foreign Minister, Robert Schuman, and it became known as the Schuman Plan. Following its announcement negotiations began which resulted, in April 1951, in the signing of the Treaty of Paris between Belgium, France, Italy, Luxembourg, the Netherlands, and West Germany. This Treaty, which came into force in August 1952, organised a common market in coal and steel, and provided for the development and control of the industries by the European Coal and Steel Community with the aims of promoting economic growth, employment, and the improvement of the standard of living in the member states. The treaty set up a High Authority as the main administrative body of the Community, with a common assembly to allow for the expression of parliamentary opinion, a consultative committee, a Council of Ministers and a Court of Justice. After the foundation of the EEC and Euratom the European Parliament replaced the Assembly and served all three communities, as did the European Court of Justice. In 1965 a further treaty merged the High Authority with the Commission of the European Community and also merged the two Councils of Ministers. The Community, enlarged following the Treaty of Accession in 1972, continues to operate under the Treaty of Paris.

The European Community

European Community. This phrase is used to describe the association of Belgium, Denmark, France, Ireland, Italy, Luxembourg, the Netherlands, West Germany, and the United Kingdom within the framework of the European Economic Community, the European Coal and Steel Community and Euratom.

European Communities Act — United Kingdom. This law, passed in 1972, brought the Treaties which created the European Community into effect in the United Kingdom. It provided for all the Community legislation that had been passed since the foundation of the community to take effect within the United Kingdom, and, as the Treaties require, said that future Community legislation should become directly applicable within the United Kingdom as if it were national law.

European Council. Meetings of the heads of Government of the member states of the European Community were held in the Hague in 1969, in Paris in 1972, in Denmark in 1973, and in Paris in 1974. At this meeting it was decided that such meetings should be held regularly, at least three times a year and they were given the title 'European Council'. A meeting of the European Council usually takes place in the country of the member state holding the Presidency of the Council of Ministers during their six months period of office.

Finances of the European Community. The European Coal and Steel Community is financed by a levy on coal and steel production. The European Economic Community and Euratom were initially financed through contributions from the member states. However, in 1970 the Council of Ministers decided that the Community should move towards a system which would provide finance from the Community's 'own resources'. These should be the proceeds from levies on agricultural imports and from customs duties on goods entering the Community, and also an amount equal to what would be raised by the imposition of value added tax on a uniform basis throughout the Community at a rate which may not exceed one per cent. The development of the process by which the Community thus acquires funds 'automatically' has strengthened the movement for greater democratic control of Community activity.

Fisheries Policy in the European Community. As a common agricultural policy for the European Community developed it seemed that a policy that organised equal access for all Community member states to all fishing grounds under the control of the various member states and the institution of a common market dealing with fish was a natural corollary to it. A common fisheries policy was agreed by the six original member states in 1971. The issue was controversial from the start of the negotiations for enlargement of the Community, and played a large part in the defeat of the proposal that Norway should join the Community. It remains controversial, particularly over matters such as the access of Community fishermen to foreign territorial waters, a question now handled on behalf of the Community as a whole, and over the right of the member states to preserve national fishing zones and to take unilateral measures to preserve fish stocks.

Languages in the European Community. The European Community has no official language. Documents and legislation are produced in the official languages of all the member states (except Gaelic into which only the most important documents are translated). Interpretation facilities are provided in Danish, Dutch, English, French, German and Italian.

Lomé Convention. In February 1975 forty-six African, Caribbean and Pacific countries signed an agreement with the European Community. Other similar states, the Seychelles for instance, have adhered to the agreement on independence. The convention provides for duty free entry into the Community of most imports from the associated states, and set up the Stabex scheme which is designed to stabilise the income received from certain basic commodities despite the fluctuations of world markets, and the European Development Fund which provides development aid.

Merger Treaty. The institutions of the European Economic Community and Euratom were to some extent modelled upon those of the European Coal and Steel Community, and in 1965 a Treaty was signed, which came into force in July 1969, which established a single Commission and Council of Ministers for all three communities. Each community however continues to operate under the rules laid down by the individual treaty which established it.

Nine, the. This phrase is sometimes used to refer to the present members of the European Community, i.e. Belgium, Denmark, France, Italy, Ireland, Luxembourg, the Netherlands, West Germany and the United Kingdom.

Paris, Treaty of. This Treaty, signed in 1951, set up the European Coal and Steel Community which came into being in August 1952. It laid down quite detailed provisions for the operation of the Community and provided the High Authority (now replaced, under the Merger Treaty, by the Commission) with some considerable executive powers to implement them. It also provided, from the start, for an independent income for the Community, raised by levies on the industry.

Political Cooperation within the European Community. The treaties which are the basis of the European Community do not provide for cooperation between the member states on matters such as foreign policy and defence. However, following the meetings of heads of government of the Six in the Hague in 1969, a committee was set up under Viscount Etienne Davignon of Belgium, which resulted in the 'Davignon' system of political cooperation. This involves regular meetings of officials of the nine member states, and of their Foreign Ministers. Technically these meetings fall outside the scope of the Community, and the Commission therefore are only involved when specifically Community matters are discussed.

Regulations of the European Community. This is the form which European Community legislation usually takes; the corresponding type of law in the European Coal and Steel Community is called a decision. Regulations are enacted by the Council of Ministers on the basis of proposals from the Commission, and after receiving the advice of the European Parliament (which they are not obliged to heed). These laws take effect directly in the member states, and are enforced by the national courts of each member state.

Rome, Treaty of. This Treaty established the European

Economic Community. It was signed in Rome in March 1957. The Treaty establishing Euratom was signed at the same time. It is often regarded as an 'outline' Treaty, envisaging the future working out of common policies rather than laying down detailed provisions for their operation. The preamble to the Treaty speaks of laying the foundations for an ever closer union amongst the peoples of Europe. Economic means are envisaged as the way towards this, with the aim of eventually eliminating all the effects of political boundaries between them on the economic activity of member states. The achievement of a common market and the maintenance of free competition within it are specified as important, and agriculture, transport, social policy, commercial policy and relations with overseas countries and territories are all mentioned as areas in which the Community should develop.

Site of the Institutions of the European Community. Brussels is the main centre of the activity of the European Community. The secretariat of the Council of Ministers is based there and the Council meets there for nine months of the year. In April, June and October it meets in Luxembourg. The Commission headquarters, the Berlaymont building, is in Brussels, though some of its staff work elsewhere, for example in Luxembourg. The European Parliament has its secretariat and a chamber in Luxembourg, but its main sessions are held in France, at Strasbourg. The European Court of Justice sits in Luxembourg, the Economic and Social Committee meets in Brussels.

Six, the. This phrase is sometimes used to refer to the original six members of the European Coal and Steel Community who were also founder members of the European Economic Community and Euratom. They are Belgium, France, Italy, Luxembourg, the Netherlands and West Germany.

Snake (in a Tunnel), the. This picturesque phrase is a description of the graphic representation of the effects of decisions taken by certain member states about exchange rates between their currencies. In 1971 and 1972 they decided that fluctuations in exchange rates between their currencies should be confined within a narrow band — 'the snake'. This narrow band would move within a wider band of maximum permitted fluctuations against the United States dollar — 'the tunnel'. The scheme had barely started in 1972 before Denmark, Ireland and the United Kingdom withdrew, under pressure from the mounting international monetary crisis. Continuing international crises and pressures from, for instance, differing rates of inflation in the various countries have meant that various attempts to solve exchange rate problems have had to be made since the early 1970s.

Unit of Account of the European Community. In order to avoid having to express every monetary figure in nine different currencies the Community uses a standard measure of monetary value. Originally this was fixed at the equivalent of an amount of gold which, before 1971, equalled the value of one United States dollar. More recently, and in the first place for the Development Fund set up under the Lomé Convention, the value of the unit of account has been calculated on the basis of a collection (basket) of certain fixed amounts of each member state's currency. The value of this unit of account against each member state's individual currency is fixed daily. This 'basket' unit of account is now becoming widely used for accounting and budgeting purposes within the Community.

Veto. The Treaties which established the European Community provide that there must be unanimity within the Council of Ministers for a decision to admit a new member state, and if the Council wish to amend a proposal made by the Commission against the Commission's wishes. On these matters each member state thus effectively possesses a right of veto. This right does not formally exist on any other matter, though at the time of the Luxembourg Accords in 1966 France made it clear that she was not prepared to accept the result of a vote in the Council of Ministers if it appeared to affect a vital national interest, and Britain has also taken this view. Indeed the British Government's undertaking to the Westminster Parliament that it will not agree to the passage of proposals which Parliament has rejected rests upon this basis.

Chapter 3

The European Parliament

Introduction

During the coming election, the organisation and powers of the European Parliament will be referred to by both the press and politicians more than ever before. This chapter asks the key questions that are sure to be at the heart of many arguments.

What is the background to the European Parliament?

Although referred to in the Treaties governing the European Communities as 'the Assembly', the main consultative body of the Communities adopted the title 'European Parliament' in 1962 and is now generally known by that name. The Parliament was included amongst the institutions of the Communities in order that the Parliamentary representatives of the 'peoples of the States brought together in the Community' (European Coal and Steel Community Treaty Article 20) should have a voice in the functioning of the Communities. Seats are distributed between the member states roughly in accordance with the size of their populations. However, because of the large differences in size between, for example, Luxembourg and France, the exact numbers reflect a compromise between the need to ensure that even the smallest have adequate representation and the need to see that the Parliament is a workable size.

The Treaties initially provided that members of the European Parliament should be designated from amongst their own members by the Parliaments of the Member States, but the EEC Treaty also provides that the Parliament shall draw up proposals for its own direct election by universal suffrage. A system of direct election has now been agreed by the Council of Ministers, and ratified by all the member states. Many people hope that the advent of direct elections will increase democratic control over the workings of the various institutions of the Communities. Others, especially in Britain and France, fear that a directly elected Parliament may seek to increase its powers at the expense of national Governments and Parliaments. Any changes in the Parliament's powers would, however, involve changes in the Treaties, which would have to be agreed by all the member states and ratified in each country.

When was the European Parliament founded?
The European Coal and Steel Community Treaty was signed in April 1951. The Community was set up in August 1952. The Treaty establishing the Community provided, in Article 20, for the establishment of an Assembly which met for the first time on 10 September 1952. In 1958, when the European Economic Community and Euratom were set up, the Treaties establishing them also provided for an Assembly, and it was agreed (and laid down by the Common Institutions Convention, signed at the same time as the Treaties) that the same Assembly should serve all three Communities. The Assembly decided in 1962 to take the title 'Parliament'. By the time that the first directly elected Parliament meets the institution will thus have been in existence for over a quarter of a century. It was enlarged when Britain, Ireland and Denmark joined the Communities in 1973.

What is the legal basis of the European Parliament?
The establishment and powers of the European Parliament rest upon the various Treaties — the European Coal and Steel Community Treaty (the Treaty of Paris), the European Economic Community Treaty (the Treaty of Rome), the Euratom Treaty — and two further treaties which extended its powers in the budgetary field — the Treaty of Luxembourg of April 1970 and a Treaty signed in Brussels in 1975. All these Treaties were international agreements which had to be ratified by each signatory state. They define the formal powers of the Parliament which will not change after direct elections. Both Britain and France now have laws saying that any change in the European Parliament's formal powers must be agreed to by an Act of Parliament.

Who are the members of the European Parliament now?
Until direct elections the European Parliament will have 198

members. All of them are also members of their national Parliaments. Thirty-six members each come from France, Germany, Italy and the United Kingdom. Both Belgium and the Netherlands send fourteen members, Denmark and Ireland send ten and Luxembourg six. The British delegation consists of eighteen Labour members, sixteen Conservatives, one Liberal and one member of the Scottish National Party. Ten of these members are members of the House of Lords, and twenty-six are members of the House of Commons.

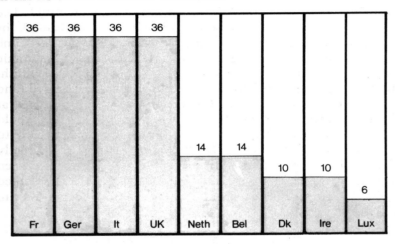

Figure 1 The present European Parliament.

What is the 'dual mandate'?
Until direct elections only members of national Parliaments have been members of the European Parliament. They have thus had a double (dual) function or mandate, both in their national Parliament and at European level.

How have members been chosen up till now?
They have been selected by their national Parliaments. In Belgium and the Netherlands, as in the United Kingdom, they are nominated from both Houses of Parliament, so as broadly to reflect the balance of parties within the Parliaments. In Germany they are chosen on a similar basis but only from the lower house of the Parliament. In France and Italy they are chosen by a majority vote in both houses, and in Luxembourg

47

the Parliament's committee for foreign and military affairs chooses them. A member who loses his seat in his national Parliament does not continue as a member of the European Parliament.

What changes will there be in the composition of the Parliament after direct elections?

After direct elections the European Parliament will be larger, 410 members in all. The United Kingdom, France, West Germany and Italy will each send eighty-one members, the Netherlands will send twenty-five, Belgium twenty-four, Denmark will send sixteen, Ireland fifteen and Luxembourg six.

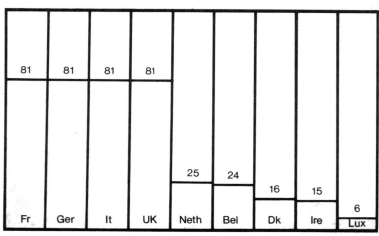

Figure 2 The composition of the enlarged Parliament.

How will the new members be elected?

The Treaties require that directly elected members should be elected by universal suffrage. However, for the first elections each country is free to choose its own way of organising this. It is hoped that a uniform system may be worked out for later elections. The United Kingdom will be the only member state to have single member constituencies whose member will be chosen on the basis of a simple majority (the 'first-past-the-post' system). All the other member states are adopting some form of proportional representation with multi-member constituencies. In Ireland there will be four constituencies, whereas, in France the whole country will be treated as a single constituency, and in Germany there will be a mixed system; some members will represent the whole country, and others will be chosen to represent each of the states (*Länder*) of the federation.

How long will members of the European Parliament remain in office?
The European Parliament has a fixed term of five years. The second direct elections will be in 1984.

Where does the European Parliament meet?
The Parliament's administrative headquarters are in Luxembourg and some of its sessions are held there. Most of its sittings, however, take place in Strasbourg. Its specialised committees may meet elsewhere, and frequently do so in Brussels. The possibility of moving the Parliament entirely to Brussels, close to the main centres of the Community's other institutions, has been raised.

When does the European Parliament meet?
The Parliamentary year of the European Parliament starts in March. During the year it usually meets about once a month (not in August) for about a week at a time. In 1977 it held thirteen such sessions. Parliamentary Committees meet more frequently.

Does the European Parliament have a Speaker?
The Parliament has a President, who presides over its sittings and who also presides over the bodies which organise the Parliament's business and its agenda. He is re-elected each year. At present the President is Emilio Colombo from Italy.

How do the Members sit?
The Members of the European Parliament do not sit facing each other but arranged in a semicircle facing the President. They do not sit together in national delegations, but according to the political group to which they belong.

What parties are represented in the European Parliament?
Since each member of the European Parliament is a member of a political party in his own country, and each country has

different parties, there may be representatives of over forty parties in the European Parliament. However, from the earliest days of the Coal and Steel Community's Assembly, members have tended to group themselves together with members of parties from other countries who share the same political outlook. These political groups, if they contain more than fourteen members (or ten members if they come from three or more different countries), are officially recognised and given a secretariat paid for from the Parliament's funds. The official spokesmen of the political groups are called to speak first in debates, and the chairmen of the groups have a voice in the organisation of the Parliament's business and in choosing the chairmen and spokesmen for the Parliamentary committees. At present there are six groups. The largest is the Socialist group with sixty-six members. The Christian Democrat group has fifty-three members, the Liberals and Democrats twenty-three, the Conservatives eighteen, the Communists and their allies eighteen, and the European Progressive Democrats sixteen. Four members are not attached to any group.

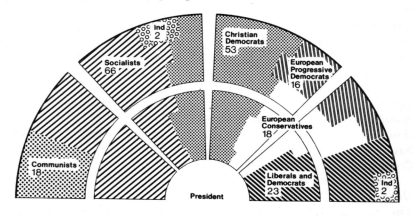

Figure 3 The seating of the political groups in the European Parliament.

Who pays the members of the European Parliament?
The Government of each member state will pay the Members of the European Parliament representing that country a salary equal to that received by members of the national Parliament. Expenses will be paid from the European Parliament's own funds which come out of the European Communities' budget.

How is Parliamentary business organised?
Unlike national parliaments, where the government or the dominant political party arrange the business of the Houses, the European Parliament is not organised by any political group. It has a 'bureau' composed of the President and twelve vice-presidents, sometimes enlarged by the attendance of the six party-group leaders, which determines the agenda and other details of the running of the sessions.

What are the European Parliament's Committees?
Like many of the parliaments in the member states (but not the United Kingdom) and British local authorities, the European Parliament has specialised standing committees, which broadly reflect the overall national and party political composition of the Parliament as a whole. At present there are twelve such Committees, which meet frequently, often in Brussels. They cover political affairs; legal affairs; economic and monetary affairs; budgets; social affairs, employment and education; agriculture; regional policy; the environment, public health and consumer affairs; energy and research; external economic relations; development and cooperation. Each of these committees has thirty-five members. The Rules of Procedure and Petitions Committee has eighteen members.

How do the specialised standing Committees work?
The specialised standing committees have two main functions. Firstly, and most importantly, they consider all proposals for Community legislation before the full session of the Parliament debates them. They produce a report on each proposal, which is presented to the full session by a spokesman (rapporteur) and includes a draft resolution expressing an opinion on the proposal. Members of the staff of the Commission, which is responsible for drafting legislative proposals, attend the appropriate Committee sessions. The second function of the

51

specialised Committees is to hold investigations and enquiries into particular problems and policies, which may include inviting witnesses to give evidence. The Committees are also often consulted by the Commission informally while it is formulating proposals for legislation. Committee meetings are not normally open to the public, and their proceedings are not published.

What happens at a plenary debate of the European Parliament?
The report of the specialised Committee on the proposal under consideration is introduced by the Committee's rapporteur. The official spokesmen of the political groups are then called to speak. Thereafter there is general debate, and a vote is taken on a resolution expressing the Parliament's opinion on the proposal, which may include suggested amendments to it.

Can the European Parliament make laws?
No. European Community laws are made by the Council of Ministers on the basis of proposals by the Commission. When

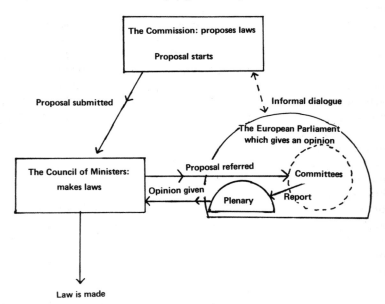

Figure 4   How Community Law is Made.
Source: European Parliament Office.

Does the European Parliament make decisions about taxes?

the Council receives proposals from the Commission it sends them to the European Parliament which sends its opinion back to the Council before the law is passed. If the Parliament's opinion differs greatly from the original proposal it may form the basis for an amended proposal submitted by the Commission to the Council. However, the Council of Ministers is not obliged to take any account of the Parliament's opinion when it makes the law.

Can the European Parliament control the other Communities' institutions?

The European Parliament has the right to dismiss the Commission. It can only dismiss all thirteen members of the Commission together, and there must be a two-thirds majority in favour of doing so, with at least half of all the Parliament's members actually voting for the dismissal of the Commission. The Parliament has never exercised this right, which is an essentially negative one, as the Parliament has no say in the appointment of Commissioners, who are appointed by agreement between the national governments of the member states. The Parliament has no control over the Council of Ministers, who actually make Communities' laws, except in certain budgetary matters.

Can the European Parliament control the Community Budget?

The Treaties of Luxembourg (1970) and Brussels (1975) gave Parliament increased rights over the budget of the European Communities. The Parliament may now take the final decision on about a quarter of the total expenditure of the Communities, lowering the expenditure proposed, or, more usually, raising it within certain agreed limits. In addition to this power over the so-called non-obligatory expenditure, the European Parliament has the right to reject the budget as a whole, which would oblige the Commission and the Council of Ministers to produce a new one. However, before this stage is reached there is a formal conciliation procedure designed to enable the Parliament and the Council to resolve differences over the budget or legislation with budgetary consequences.

Does the European Parliament make decisions about taxes?

No. Unlike the budget in the Westminster Parliament, which is used as an instrument of general economic policy and is concerned with raising as well as spending money, the Communities' budget is essentially concerned with estimated expenditure on Communities' policies and institutions. The money to pay for this expenditure is raised partly from the proceeds of customs duties and agricultural levies, upon the level of which the Council of Ministers decides, and partly by contributions from member states. From 1979 these contributions are due to be replaced by the payment to the Community of a proportion of the Value Added Tax raised by the member states. However, the extent of the current contributions, and the actual size of the proportion of VAT to be paid (it may not exceed the equivalent of a one per cent VAT rate) are, and will continue to be, decided by the Council of Ministers.

Can members of the European Parliament ask parliamentary questions?
Yes. Members of the European Parliament may ask both oral and written questions both of the Commission and of the Council of Ministers. Since 1973 there has been a one-and-a-half hour question-time on the second or third day of each sitting when members may follow up their initial questions with supplementary questions. In 1977 the Commission answered 1,013 written and 59 oral questions from members of the European Parliament.

Are there 'adjournment debates'?
In the Westminster Parliament these are short debates on some specific topical or local issue or problem. In the European Parliament these take the form of oral questions with debate, which may be put by a political group, one of the specialised committees, or at least five members together.

What language do the members of the European Parliament use in debates?
Six languages may officially be used in debates and all the European Parliament's documents are translated into each of them. Simultaneous translation into each of them is available during all debates. The languages are English, French, German, Italian, Dutch and Danish.

Will the powers of the European Parliament be increased?

Is there a European Parliament 'Hansard'?
'Hansard' is a verbatim record of what happens in the Houses of Parliament each day, produced the following day. A verbatim record of this kind is produced for the European Parliament, giving each contribution in its original language. An official text of the proceedings of the Parliament translated into English appears about a month later.

Will the powers of the European Parliament be increased after direct elections?
The powers of the European Parliament are defined by the Treaties which form its legal basis. These powers can only be increased by alterations to the Treaties, which would have to be made by further treaties. After direct elections, therefore, formally there will be no change. However, many people expect that an enlarged and directly elected Parliament will become more vigorous, expanding its activities within the present limits and possibly pressing for the extension of those limits. Such possibilities have already been discussed. In 1972 a Committee set up by the Commission of the European Communities under the French academic and lawyer, Professor Georges Wedel, recommended for example that in some areas both the Parliament and the Council of Ministers should have to assent to a proposal before it became law. These suggestions have not been implemented.

Chapter 4

The Background to the Direct Elections

Introduction

The story of British involvement in Direct Elections to the European Parliament predated the Referendum (see p. 21) by over a year. However, as the permanence of Britain's EEC membership was in doubt until after June 1975, the achievements reached before then were effectively shelved. Thus Britain's early influence was one which continued a long tradition of delay over this issue, dating back to the first Draft Convention of 1960. Over the actual passing of the Direct Elections Act, Britain's record was equally dilatory. In terms of the time taken between the passing of the September 1976 Act and the completion of ratification in member states, Britain took the longest (with 17 months) despite the fact that the original enabling legislation had been included in the Queen's speech of November 1976.[1] Britain's legislation was also unique in that the majority in the House of Commons was the smallest of any lower House in Europe. It is possible to provide a number of interpretations of the fact that Britain's enthusiasm did not match that of her partners.

Special Problems in Britain

Firstly, it is not difficult to see that Britain was in a rather special position on three counts: the effect of the recent Referendum, the economic situation, and the balance of parties in Parliament. By the middle of June 1975, for example, prices were 26% higher than they had been a year before, major groups of workers were still gaining increases of around 30% and sterling had fallen nearly 4% in the previous six weeks. While the economic situation was serious enough to concentrate minds most wonderfully on the crisis at home, it was also instrumental in further aggravating divisions within the Labour

56

Party and Government. Continual cries from the Left for
import controls obviously meant that whatever the result of the
Referendum had been, disagreements would remain European
as well as domestic, given the ever increasing levels of EEC
imports.

The referendum, characterised as it was by the abandonment
of collective responsibility, was seen as having two possible
effects on Labour anti-marketeers. A large 'Yes' vote could have
quieted their opposition, proving that they were not speaking
for the mass of people, or their position could have been seen as
so entrenched that defeat could not repair divisions in the
party. Although the referendum had settled, for the time being
at least, the question of Britain's membership, it did not, as so
many have pointed out subsequently, give a mandate for the
Direct Elections specifically. Therefore, much of the debate was
to hinge on whether EEC membership and accession to the
Treaties involved were, in fact, inseparable from a commitment
to Direct Elections. This was not a new debate in Europe.
Indeed, the French attitude, under Gaullist influence, had long
been critical of the underlying basis of Direct Elections and
their role in relation to national sovereignty and the power of
national parliaments. However, the British, new as they were
upon the scene, were in effect reopening an old issue which had
received considerable attention in Europe for the previous
fifteen years and was entering its dying phases in all but the
Gaullist and some Communist camps.

Another very British characteristic which was a late entrant
compared with the two above, was the state of the arithmetic
in Parliament by the beginning of 1977. The Lib-Lab pact,
formed in order to prevent either Labour or the Liberals having
to face a potentially disastrous election in the spring of 1977,
had a number of founding principles. Prominent amongst these
was the passing of the Direct Elections legislation on time and
with the use of a proportional system of election. In hindsight,
such an arrangement may well have been a mixed blessing in
terms of its effect on Britain's behaviour over Direct Elections.
From the point of view of timing, it is likely that a Conservative
Cabinet would have found it easier to introduce and pass the
legislation in time for the original election date of May or June
1978. However, for supporters of proportional representation,
the Tory leadership would have been an even worse bet than

the Labour Government. While the Liberals certainly came to the rescue at a time when the first Bill was unlikely to succeed, they also turned the debate into one of the most extensive reviews of electoral systems which Britain had seen since the 1918 Representation of the People Bill. Equally, the precarious situation of the Government, caught as it was between its own dissenters and the evangelical zeal of the PR lobby, meant that the Second Bill which was introduced left many of the contentious questions wide open.[2] This was most true of the electoral system, thus preventing an embarrassing spectacle of the Government's front and back benchers trooping into the wrong lobby under a three line whip in the face of their 'allies', the Liberals. This not only delayed the legislation still further but also gave an impression of both weakness and indecision on the part of the Government to European observers. With the absence of any Parliamentary majority for PR, the impact of the Lib-Lab pact produced a very British (as opposed to 'European') type of debate, rather than a change of heart. Issues which had been important in Europe, such as national weighting, were subsumed under preoccupation with electoral systems: regionally, with the case of Northern Ireland and the continuation of overrepresentation of Scotland and Wales; and nationally, over the overall choice of system.

These factors might, therefore, explain why it was that Britain was less than helpful in reaching the original target date for the first direct elections. But the broad terms of 'Referendum', 'Economic Crisis' and 'Parliamentary Balance', while all very British and very relevant, cannot stand as explanations in themselves. Indeed, an alternative interpretation is available from a Hansard Society publication of 1977, under the title of *The British People and their Voice in Europe*, whose general conclusions over Britain's role in Europe can be adapted to this more specialised issue. Their suggestion that Britain was spending so much time on old battles that there was little energy or enthusiasm left for things European can well be applied to the political parties involved, showing that direct elections were instrumental in disinterring party skeletons across the board.

The Passage of the Direct Elections Bill

The Labour Party, as the party of Government, was shouldered with the responsibility of implementing what was seen, by the leadership at least, as a Treaty obligation and could therefore be an easy target for the allocation of praise or blame in delaying the process. What the Referendum had shown was not so much a sudden upsurge in anti-market opinion within the party but the continuation of strong opposition from the Left which had originated when Europe was still a twinkle in Adenauer's eye. Nothing had changed since then except that more anti-marketeers had more positions of power in the Party and the Government, producing numerous leaks in the press of dissent in the Cabinet. It was to provoke this speech from William Whitelaw in the House,

I am simply pointing out that the Government, who procrastinated and delayed, certainly at the wish of their own supporters, have no right now to come along and tell Parliament 'You have got to pass it all very urgently. It has nothing to do with us if we fail to meet the target date in 1978.' The Secretary of State knows perfectly well that he is going to try to blame other people . . .[3]

The situation had certainly been made very difficult for Wilson, who had adopted a rather qualified pro-European stance during the Referendum by diverting debate from membership to its terms for Britain, and later for Callaghan who had taken on the role of making sure that Britain played its part without necessarily making it an easy or a joyful task. The free vote on the Second Reading of the first Direct Elections Bill in July 1977 showed the extent of the problem with one-third of the Cabinet, half the other Ministers and a good majority of backbench MPs either voting against or abstaining. (See Chapter 5)

This was a very similar voting pattern to that of April 1975 on whether to accept the renegotiated terms for British membership. The combination of a prolonged and public hearing having been given to irreconcilable differences within the party and continued difficulties of the leadership in maintaining a credible stance over Europe, meant that personal, party and national allegiances were severely strained. On these, if on no other grounds, the Labour Government can be excused for not finding Direct Elections legislation a particularly relishing prospect. Indeed, one observer, Michael Stewart, has described the European issue as capable of splitting the Labour Party, 'rendering it impotent for a decade, and, perhaps, destroying it altogether'.[4]

For the Conservative Party, the skeleton was not one of

divided loyalties as such, at least, not over Europe. Unlike Harold Wilson, Edward Heath could never be accused of having changed his mind over Europe or of being lukewarm in his support once it was established. Despite the presence of a number of anti-market Conservative MPs and the nuisance of a former Tory Minister, Enoch Powell, producing highly lucid vilification of Direct Elections both inside Parliament and out, the real problem was that of the party leadership. The liberal wing of the party headed by its ex-leader, Heath, supported the use of proportional representation, not only on the grounds of equity of representation but also as an essentially pro-European move, their enthusiasm for the rapid completion of 'European Unity' being on the whole stronger than elsewhere in the party. Mrs. Thatcher, on the other hand, supported by the great majority of Tory MPs, felt that the advantage which the traditional system of election gave to the two major parties was too great a sacrifice for European Unity, especially since, in the words of one Tory member, it was unnecessary to change the system for the first round since it was likely to be changed for the second anyway.

The Economist[5] suggested that no more than 70 Tory MPs were in favour of the regional list system by 16 July 1977 and in the Labour Party 120 MPs were in favour. So, despite the likelihood of resounding defeat in the vote, the discussions about PR in the Conservative Party were all the more furious for the fact that the retention of the traditional system was seen as being at best a touch of the 'Little Englander' mentality and at worst confirmation of a move to the right in the party since the removal of Heath. The PR proponents also pointed out that fears of it automatically leading to PR at Westminster elections were unfounded and that the time required for the drawing up and verification of 'first-past-the-post' constituencies would be sufficient to make that choice of system a delaying tactic itself. All this, of course, was like the battle being waged along the same lines for the party leadership. It was made all the more uncomfortable by the fact that the PR supporters chose a public forum rather than a private squabble. Consequently, in the press, in Parliament and in party circles, the arguments over the choice of electoral system went round and round, largely because they were concerned with more than just an electoral system or Direct Elections.

The Passage of the Direct Elections Bill

Within the Liberal Party, it is clear that consistency of purpose and Parliamentary party unity were stronger here than in either of the two above. Given that they had everything to gain and nothing to lose if direct elections were quickly implemented and by a proportional system of election, such virtues were more of an inevitability than an achievement. The Liberals, of course, were constantly underrepresented in Westminster and elsewhere. Their proffering of arguments in favour of a change of system, their explanation of the various alternatives, and their education of the broader public, was kept up with great energy and vigour. In fact, for a party which was undergoing a decline in popularity over other issues the Liberals seemed to be closely in line with public opinion on Direct Elections and Electoral Systems. By July 1977, 40% of the British public thought that the EEC was a 'bad thing' while 35% thought it was a 'good thing', whereas 67% were in favour of Direct Elections and 22% were against.[6] On electoral systems, an ORC poll of April 1977 had shown that while 55% were in favour of PR for the Direct Elections, 74% were in favour of it for Westminster elections. Certainly, in a European context, the exclusion of a party with 18.3% of the vote in a previous national election from any representation in Europe, merely because of an electoral system which was no longer in use in any other member state, would seem at best a form of gross inequity.

The smaller parties were also very much concerned with issues which were far from new. The UUUC, for example, with over half their MPs voting against the Second Reading of the Bill, certainly expressed some of the most fervent opposition to Proportional Representation since its effect in Ulster would be to ensure more representation for the SDLP. In the Nationalist parties, concern with the national status of their areas gave an added twist to what was, by European standards, a highly provincial debate in Britain.

Finally, the Bill for Direct Elections passed through its last stages in the Commons on 7 February 1978, with the Regional List system voted out and one important amendment aiming at the protection of national sovereignty put in. The opponents to the Bill, like those in the Referendum, were not only Labour's left and the Conservative right, but also a number of MPs who although moderates on other issues were strongly anti-EEC. The ranks were swelled by all the Welsh Nationalists and most of the Ulster Unionists. But just as the number of advocates of the traditional electoral system had almost pre-determined the choice of system, so the large pro-Direct Election majority meant that despite the many arguments and delays there would have been little hope of defeating the legislation in the Commons. The Boundary Commission did not publish its provisional schedule of boundaries until the summer of 1978 and given the large number of submissions for change which they received, it was obvious that the final map would be delayed. It was not in fact ready until 23 November 1978 because of problems caused by translation into Welsh and an industrial dispute at HMSO. As this had meant a wait of nine months from the completion of legislation in the Commons to the final version of Britain's constituency schedule, it is certainly true that the electoral system chosen had little to do with economy of time or effort.

The Role of the Anti-Market Lobbies

It is interesting to look at the anti-Market lobbies, both inside the two major parties and outside, in greater detail to see what it was about Direct Elections which came under fire and how much of the argument was a repeat of the Referendum debate and how much was in any sense new. The largest and loudest concentration of anti-Market feeling was on the Left of the Labour Party. There was also the faction in the Conservative Party and in the non-party national and regional anti-Common Market leagues and groups. However, these groups were not only further from the government's immediate concern and the strings of power but were also much less in the public eye, with the exception of Enoch Powell's indefatigable campaign.

Of the large number of letters, pamphlets, articles and speeches produced in the party press and independently by Labour anti-Market groups, many of the most articulate items came from the Labour Common Market Safeguards Committee which, claiming the support of 80 Labour MPs, published a pamphlet in May 1976 to commemorate the Referendum's anniversary. They quoted this in their written submission to the Select Committee on Direct Elections at the end of the same month.[7] Three basic reasons were given for their opposition to Direct Elections in principle.

1) While agreeing that the EEC required more democratic control, they felt that another tier of government at the European level and the inevitable threatening of the power of Westminster were not the correct means of achieving it.
2) They believed that the terms of Britain's membership of the EEC were thoroughly inequitable and therefore they opposed any strengthening of institutions which, by weakening the voice of individual nationalities in the EEC, would prevent any chance of Britain fighting for a better deal.
3) They felt that a more satisfactory way of achieving democratisation and national hegemony would be the strengthening of the Council of Ministers at the expense of the Commission and the Assembly.[8]

At first sight, several of these recommendations appear inconsistent if not actually contradictory. For instance, the idea that 'democratisation' could be increased by reducing the power of the Assembly and the Commission and increasing the power of the Council of Ministers is curious, given that the Council is not seen as an especially democratic organ. It often ignores the views of the Assembly and it is obvious that a conflict arises between 'democratisation' for the EEC and for the nation state. The Labour Safeguards Committee obviously believed that any democracy at the European level is impossible and the only answer is to return to the hegemony of the state and hence to reply upon the veto of a Government Minister in Brussels. Equally, 'democracy' is an increasingly ambiguous word, related as much to the government of elites by the mass of the population as it is to universal suffrage and free elections in their more restricted sense. Taking all three recommendations together, however, a thoroughly consistent picture emerges of a strong desire to retain full national sovereignty not for its own sake and as a protection for the Commonwealth as was argued in the post-war years, but because the democracy of elections and the democracy of mass control of power and resources are here seen to be in conflict.

The dislike of Direct Elections among the smaller Communist and far Left parties in Europe today and also until recently of the larger Communist parties of France and Italy show that these views are widely aired in Europe. The Left in Europe today is split between those who are trying to change the system from within and those who are fighting a rearguard action to prevent development at the European level in any form. These divisions are evident within and also between the various European parties involved. The Labour Party's position was awkward because it found it difficult to decide whether to join the European Socialist Group for the purpose of the election campaign or not.

Similar arguments have also been long used by the Gaullists whose influence was gaining momentum again in 1977, partly due to the state of the parliamentary balance in France. It is interesting to compare the amendments passed in both countries as a result of the same pressures. In Britain, the Prime Minister gave an assurance to the Parliamentary Labour Party before the vote on the guillotine motion required to get the Second Bill through, that there would be an amendment protecting the sovereignty of Britain and Westminster included in the Bill. This amendment was introduced by David Owen on 26 January 1977 and was passed on 2 February in Committee by 101 votes to 7, reading as follows:

No treaty which provides for any increase in the powers of the Assembly shall be ratified by the United Kingdom unless it has been approved by an Act of Parliament. In this section 'treaty' includes any international agreement and any protocol or annex to a treaty or international agreement.[9]

In France, the process was rather more involved. In response to pressure from both Gaullists and some Communists, the issue was referred to a Constitutional Council to discover if any constitutional objections existed to the implementation of Direct Elections legislation. Although the report of 30 December 1976 showed that no such objections could be raised, they defined French national sovereignty in such a restrictive sense as to make it impossible for any extension in the powers of the European Assembly or any development towards federalism in Europe without a constitutional amendment. This lead to the following stipulation in the second Article of the ratification Bill:

Any modification of the powers of the European Parliament, such as they were established at the date of the signature of the Act providing for the election of representatives to the Parliament by direct universal suffrage (i.e. 20 September 1976) which had not been ratified or approved according to the provisions of the Treaties of Paris and Rome and which, in such a case had not given rise to a revision of the constitution in conformity with the decision of the Constitutional Council of 30 December 1976 would be null and void as regards France. The same would apply to any act of the European Parliament which, without being founded on a specific modification of its powers, surpassed them in fact.[10]

The major difference between the two amendments is that, having a written constitution, the French will allow increases in the powers of the European Parliament only with a Constitutional Amendment whereas in Britain the equivalent barrier is the need to pass legislation. Less obviously, the French amendment appears to be much more subtle and understanding in its handling of the European Parliament. In its last provision the possibility of the European Parliament using measures other than an internationally agreed protocol to increase its powers is well safeguarded against, whereas the British amendment is much more formalistic and stiff in its approach. It would appear that the longer experience of EEC affairs of the French stood them in good stead in this respect. In either case, however, the timing of any proposal to increase the powers of the European Parliament, be it formal or informal, will have to take much more careful account of the balance of pro- and anti-Market opinion in the British and French Parliaments and a very careful legal analysis of the Rome Treaty similar to that which took place in 1960, with the first real move towards Direct Elections, under pressure from the French. Neither of these provisions necessarily prevents any moves towards a more powerful Assembly but they do retain the importance of political balance at the level of the nation state rather than within the European Parliament itself, and as such are essentially conservative moves preventing a natural development of policy within the European political groupings as opposed to within the national parties. By the same token, however, these provisions should have provided a vehicle for defusing the urgency of much of the opposition in both Britain and France.

A further similarity between Labour anti-Marketeers and the Gaullists was their attempt to keep the Assembly at the same size, 198 members or roughly 1.3m voters per seat. This, according to Lord Gladwyn, 'could not be considered to be truly representative of European public opinion, and therefore could not be qualified to possess any additional powers'.[11] In this case it is the legitimacy which fully representative Direct Elections were thought to bestow upon the European Parliament, which is under attack. In other words, where it may not be possible to prevent the elections altogether they should be made an impotent exercise by whatever means are available. A second instrument of this type was the move to make the elections coincident with national elections and to make the dual mandate compulsory. This was raised in Britain and Denmark although the latter suggestion did not survive the enabling legislation. Obviously, if national elections took place at different times all over the EEC, a Europe-wide campaign would be prevented. The accompanying assets of Europe-wide publicity and an EBU election programme being put over to all the member states would be unnecessary. Equally, each European MP would have to be elected on domestic issues first in a national election thus preventing the European Parliament from providing alternative paths for political careers, and, more importantly, preventing the European MPs from having any independence from their national parties and their whips. In a European context of debate, both these devices were among the most impractical suggestions produced for the conduct of Direct Elections. It is likely that future opposition will realise that proposals which fundamentally contradict the whole purpose of a given project are not likely to succeed, whereas action at the level of national parliaments and legislation has a better chance. This change has already been reflected in Labour Party policy debates on Europe at their 1978 Conference.

A second possibility for concerted opposition to further 'federalist' moves in Europe is cooperation between groups of like mind, from different nations and different political persuasions. This 'strange bedfellow' pattern of opposition to Europe which has always been evident in both France and Britain was shown in the Safeguards Committee's proposals when they explained that they had the support of the French. In the near future, however, it is unlikely that such ad hoc cooperation would ever challenge the already well established political party groupings in Europe who currently dominate cleavages within the European Assembly. The financial assistance given to European party groupings stipulates merely that such a group must have more than one party and more than one nation represented within its ranks. Although it would not directly prevent an alliance of anti-Market opinion in such a group, it does militate against it in other ways. The current system does not necessarily produce very logical groupings. The European Progressive Democrats are one of the more curious, composed of Gaullists and Fianna Fail. The European Conservative Group is made up of British and Danish Conservatives isolated from the main group of the Right, the Christian Democrats, because of the recent association of 'Conservative' with nationalist and fascist politics in Europe. But the prospects for an anti-Market group are not good given that with the exception of the Gaullists, anti-Marketeers are located in parties which are either too small to have significant numbers of European MPs or parties which have incorporated both pro- and anti- members and hence could not produce an alliance of complete parties of sufficient strength to challenge the status quo.

The actual impact of the anti-Market lobby within the Labour Party upon the timing and conduct of Direct Elections outside the amendment above is not easy to isolate. It could be, for example, that the very limited time allowed for written memoranda to be sent to the House of Commons Select Committee hastened the process of legislation or, as is more likely, it prevented those likely to be coherent on the subject from being so and allowed the Labour Party representations to be as vague as they were with good reason.[12] Several of the written submissions, especially those from academics, referred to the impossibility of giving sufficient consideration to the subject in the time allowed and it is beyond dispute that some of the evidence given by Labour Party witnesses was less than thoroughly considered. For example, the evidence of Reg Underhill, the Labour Party National Agent, was curiously unclear on some very important issues. By July 1976 they had not decided whether to participate in a European political grouping during the campaign, what view to take of the distribution of seats within the UK, whether to make the dual mandate compulsory, what to do about double voting and voting rights of British nationals abroad, and whether there should be financial aid for the election for the parties' campaign.

As was to be expected, given the distribution of anti-Market opinion within the party, many of the points of evidence were in direct contravention to the firm ideas which the Government had put forward by this stage. Reg Underhill, thinking perhaps of the high levels of feeling in the constituency parties, suggested that rather than have Direct Elections at all: 'The Labour Party might suggest nomination throughout; therefore it is not a matter on which I would like to comment,' and when asked whether the Labour Government was committed to Direct Elections in 1978, the reply was: 'I do not know. I believe it is.'[13]

The latter might cause one to question the relationship of the Heads of government meetings with their own policies or can be taken as guidance that making any statement about commitments to Direct Elections had become so delicate as to be almost impossible. Lack of desire or ability to be especially helpful to the Select Committee was therefore certainly a result of the balance of opinion in Labour Party circles. It is possible that some of the more technical suggestions (especially the one concerning the eligibility of British nationals abroad to vote) which were produced and implemented at a later stage proved the extent of the real impact of the anti-Market lobby. The anti-European notion of preventing British voters abroad from voting either in Britain or in their country of residence, although important when contrasted to proposals in Italy, was, perhaps, an inevitable result of the influence of a group which was itself torn between non-cooperation and policy impact. Had the Government been relying on the votes of its own party to secure Direct Elections, the effects of the anti-Market group with its numbers and strength of purpose would have been much more dramatic. As it is, with little to its liking having been included in the Bill, there were signs that the next leadership campaign within the party would prove a better vehicle for anti-Market sympathy, with Tony Benn already organising an anti-EEC platform for the purpose.

Turning to the anti-Market faction within the Conservative Party a startling contrast emerges between them and their much better organised counterparts in France. One factor in this must have been the effect of Edward Heath's leadership, which had made 'Europe' a very important part of Conservative policy. Heath, like many others of an earlier vintage, viewed the EEC as a bulwark against excessive statism in Britain. The votes taken on Britain's original entry into the EEC show that even under his leadership the Tory ranks were certainly not united. There had been ministerial resignations such as those of Jasper More and Edward Taylor.[14] In addition there were about 35 Tory MPs obviously against entry despite a Conservative Conference vote of 8 to 1 in favour. However, there was not then, nor is there now, a well-organised Conservative group with firm backing in Parliament opposed to the EEC and the likelihood of a leadership campaign being fought on this issue alone is less than remote. Equally, unlike the Gaullists in France, nationalism, anti-Americanism and national hegemony had not been central planks of the Tories' policies or image. What had in the post-war era been Churchill's three circles of the Commonwealth, the Atlantic alliance and Europe had changed by 1970 to become in Heath's eyes at least, Europe at almost any cost, a continuing commitment to NATO and the Commonwealth coming a rather poor third. This was shown by Heath's support of arms sales to South Africa in the face of Kaunda's threat that Britain should be expelled from the Commonwealth if she did. While a change of leadership has meant a lessening in outright 'federalism' fervour on the Tory front bench, it has not been accompanied by a strengthening of outright anti-Market opinion in any way equivalent with that in the Labour Party, despite the obvious realisation in the party of the need to respond to the EEC's unpopularity in the country.

This is not to say that no opposition to Direct Elections was produced from Conservative organs. The Conservative Trident group, being explicitly anti-Market in a letter published in 1976, disagreed with Direct Elections on the basis of a vague defence of 'Britishness' and more specific adherence to the value of sovereignty, concluding with '. . . as Britishers we have the right to be governed by Britishers from Westminster. The recent Referendum on the Common Market clearly did *not* give to Parliament any mandate to enter into any sort of Federal structure.'[15] Here are two very important arguments which were to be much in evidence in the Second Reading Debates of 1977, namely, the questioning of the Government's mandate for such legislation and the domino idea of one thing leading to another in Europe. However, as has already been shown, these arguments were an equal prerogative of the Left. The potentially powerful ammunition in the wording of Article 138 of the Rome Treaty, which stipulated a 'uniform procedure' and which was shown to be giving the Assembly the obligation to draw up proposals rather than the member states the obligation to implement them, was fired to little effect.

The tactics of the Tory anti-Marketeers, impotent as they were by comparison with those of the Left, were shown largely in the parliamentary debates. The contributions were varied indeed, ranging from Neil Marten's raising of a number of points of order and interrupting William Whitelaw, amongst others, to that of Ian Gow, who explained: 'I am an unashamed Gaullist' in the middle of a lengthy speech.[16] His is an interesting example since he had voted 'yes' in the Referendum and yet here referred to an increasing distance he felt from his own front bench. In combining a number of obviously Gaullist arguments about 'Europe des Patries', he produced a more British argument about overgovernment, remoteness and weighty bureaucracies adding his own version of the three circles, the UN, NATO and Europe, pointing out that neither of the first two required election of their representatives.[17] Another dissenting Tory, Nick Budgen, expressed the fear that the Direct Elections would produce a campaign cutting across party lines in a federal Europe versus nation-state type of battle. This is not an argument which has been widely aired and in fact requires greater consideration.

In terms of the selection of candidates, for example, the two major parties will be in different situations, given Labour's well organised anit-Market lobby. However, the problems of anti-Marketeers will be similar from wherever they come. Their selection in the constituency parties will have to be made in the knowledge that most of the 'pro' votes in the constituency will be lost to another party. Despite the decreasing popularity of the EEC since the Referendum, neither of the major parties is likely to organise an official 'out' campaign for the election meaning that anti-Market candidates will have the dual problem of probably opposing their party's manifesto and of being accused of hypocrisy in seeking election to a body of which they thoroughly disapprove. This may prevent the electors from giving a clear 'pro' or 'anti' result in the election but it will certainly produce strain within the parties and here, with the possible exception of the UUUC and the SNP, the Labour party will be worse off vis-à-vis the rest.

Another, more unusual argument was produced by John Stokes MP who was sad that whereas he thought the party was right to oppose Devolution it would not oppose constitutional change in Europe's direction. Having referred to de Gaulle, Adenauer and Churchill, he concluded: 'I believe that some of my more over-enthusiastic colleagues, to whose sincerity I pay tribute, have been tactless and over-hasty in espousing the European idea and trying to merge our Britishness in some vague European mess of pottage.'[18] Whereas most Conservative criticisms are more in praise of the nation state than in retribution against the EEC (unlike those of the Left) this attitude shows a curious combination of 'Britishness' and vilification adding further variety to the views on the Tory side. Whereas the majority of their institutional and constitutional arguments are very similar to those of the Left, especially that of the almost secret incremental acquisition of power expected by the European Parliament, the Right favoured a more cultural approach relying heavily on Britain's long history of democracy leaving the Left to deal with the more searching study of what democracy would really mean in Europe. Given the different strength of opposition on both sides, it is paradoxical to note that after the elections the Labour delegation will find itself already well assimilated into the European Parliament through the work of the Labour delegations since summer 1975 whereas the Conservatives will be a large fish in a rather insignificant pond of European Conservatives compared with the main grouping of the right, the Christian Democrats.

The national and regional groups against the Common Market in their submissions to the House of Commons Select Committee of 1976 leaned more on the unusual arguments of the Right than they did upon any of those of the Left. The coincidence of the legislation with devolution, the threat of overgovernment, excessive red tape and loss of national sovereignty all featured largely. This would suggest that whereas most of the leftist opponents to Direct Elections were able to use a number of organisations of their own as a forum for criticism, the Right have had to retain the ad hoc, non-party organisation created for the Referendum campaign. On the whole, the potential for action is with the Left also, especially since the extreme Right, in the form of the National Front, is currently dominating the politics of 'Britishness', with some of their arguments being very similar to those of the Rightist anti-Marketeers, and may thus make such policies as politically unacceptable as the term 'Conservative' has become in Europe as a whole.

The fourth section of anti-Market opinion is that of a single politician, Enoch Powell, whose highly individual manner and stance prevents his inclusion in a wider group. Mr Powell's reputation for brilliant oratory in the House has rivalled even that of Michael Foot, but his learned deliveries in the Direct Election debates were especially noticeable against a number of speeches which seemed less aware of the intricacies of European Institutions. Having eschewed the tendency to immediately equate a Federal Europe with Direct Elections he pointed out that the Treaty of Rome intended *political union*, a very different thing. In the context of political union he showed that the role of Direct Elections would be crucial, since he believed that the passing of the Bill would not be so much an enabling action as one which confirmed that Europe was already a political reality and 'that we would be morally and logically committed to follow through the consequences of political union'.[19] Equally, he was very specific as to the actual powers of the European Parliament, suggesting that as the sovereignty of Westminster had been achieved through the control of the 'purse' so with its control over the Community Budget, the European Assembly was already on the road to greater power. What he omitted, in this respect, was the fact that the European Assembly's power over the Budget is rather like an atomic weapon, able as they are to vote out the Budget as a whole, but unable to make a positive contribution to its contents. Thirdly, he proffered the difficulty pertaining to EEC legislation after Direct Elections: 'After this Bill is passed, it will not be in this House, the National Parliament who, on matters concerning the EEC will confer a mandate or give the authority to the Government Front Bench.'[20] It will, in fact, be the electorate, but this was not seen by Mr. Powell as being preferable to the restoration of power to Westminster.

There have been, then, a large number of reservations about Direct Elections in the British camp. Some of the arguments are similar to those propounded elsewhere in Europe but the majority are not. There are those which are of the Right or the Left and a majority which are both. There are technical, ideological, institutional and historical arguments resulting in all manner of representations, devices and tactics, but the net result produced a Bill which was late but otherwise largely unaffected. However, the image which the Community holds of Britain certainly was affected. Representatives of the other member states even went so far as to publish a letter in *The Times*[21] on the day of the Second Reading of the Second Bill

Footnotes

pointing to the damaging effect on Britain's image if she was seen as the sole cause of delaying the elections beyond the original date. Although the Bill was passed, the lack of Government strength and the extent and nature of opposition cannot have improved Britain's chances of influence in Europe.

Footnotes

1. See *Keesing's* for details of the timing of ratification in the member states 10 March 1978, p. 28871 ff.
2. A. King *Britain says Yes*. 1977 Washington D.C. AEIPPR.
3. *Hansard*, vol 939, no 16, col 1777. Mr Whitelaw lead up to these comments amid considerable heckling; 'Given the necessary ministerial agreement, it could easily have been ready for introduction before Christmas 1976. But, of course, there was no such ministerial agreement. Instead, there was strong opposition to the introduction of any Bill at all, which led to procrastination — (Hon. Members 'Hear, Hear') I am glad to have the support of Hon. Gentlemen — and delay. (Hon. Members: 'Why not?').
4. *The Jekyll and Hyde Years: Politics and Economic Policy since 1964.* Stewart M., Dent and Sons, London 1977, p. 56.
5. *The Economist*, 16 July 1977.
6. For wider public opinion surveys concerning Direct Elections in all the member states, see *Eurobarometer* no. 7 July 1977, pp. 38 ff.
7. For their full submission to the Select Committee see p. 35 ff in the Second Report from the Select Committee on Direct Elections to the European Assembly Volume II Session 1975/6 HMSO 3/8/76.
8. See p. 36 (ibid) for the full iteration of the arguments, especially their view that the Referendum gave no mandate for Direct Elections.
9. This is described in *Keesing's* (ibid), p. 28873.
10. The build up to this amendment is also shown in *Keesing's* (ibid), pp. 28871/2.
11. See p. 62 Select Committee for Lord Gladwyn's evidence 2nd Report (ibid) — all of which is extremely well argued and interesting, unlike much of the other evidence in the report.
12. This argument really moves towards a type of conspiracy theory over the effect of anti-Marketeers in the Labour Party. Although many Conservatives felt this to be the case, that the elections were being delayed by fair means or foul, it is not possible to prove this either way.
13. See minute 488 in the Minutes of Evidence taken before the Select Committee HMSO Cmnd 462 (i-xi). See also minute 501 on the Labour Party's commitment to Direct Elections.
14. For a fuller description of this period see *'Heath and the Heathmen'* by Andrew Roth, Routledge and Kegan Paul, London 1972.
15. See p. 49 of the Second Report of the Select Committee (ibid).
16. House of Commons Debates, *Hansard*, vol 939, no 16, col 1782.
17. House of Commons Debates, *Hansard*, vol 939, no 16, cols 1859-62.

18. House of Commons Debates, *Hansard*, vol 939, no 16, cols 1851-52.
19. House of Commons Debates, *Hansard*, vol 939, no 16, col 1789.
20. Ibid, col 1791.
21. See also *The Times* for 30 October 1977, 10 October 1977 and 31 October 1977.

Chapter 5

The Voting Record:
Analysis of the Key Divisions

Introduction

This chapter contains a full analysis of the voting records of every MP on Europe in the three crucial votes in the House of Commons that were taken from October 1974 to 1977. These votes were on the renegotiated terms of membership and the two key votes on the passage of the Direct Elections Bill.

Key to the Tables

R is the vote on the Prime Minister's motion seeking approval of the renegotiated terms of British membership of the EEC, 9 April 1975. DE is the vote on the second reading of the Direct Elections Bill, 24 November 1977. PR is the vote on the method of election. In each case, X is a vote for the government, i.e. for acceptance of the terms, for direct elections, and for proportional representation rather than first-past-the-post. S denotes a Speaker or deputy who does not vote. N denotes that a member was not an MP when this vote was taken (because he had left by then, or because he had not yet been elected.) Tellers are counted as voters throughout.

* This material, originally prepared and devised by David McKie for the Guardian/Quartet Election Guide is reproduced with his generous permission. Both Macmillan and the authors warmly thank him for this permission.

TABLE 2

THE KEY DIVISIONS AT WESTMINSTER
VOTING RECORDS 1974–1977

LAB MP	Constituency	Europe R	DE	PR
Abse, L.	Pontypool	X	X	—
Allaun, F.	Salford E	—	O	O
Anderson, D.	Swansea E	X	X	X
Archer, P.	Warley W	—	X	X
Armstrong, E.	Durham NW	X	X	X
Ashley, J.	Stoke S	X	X	X
Ashton, J.	Bassetlaw	O	O	—
Atkins, R.	Preston N	O	O	O
Atkinson, N.	Tottenham	O	O	O
Bagier, G.	Sunderland S	X	X	O
Barnett, G.	Greenwich	O	—	X
Barnett, J.	Heywood	X	X	X
Bates, A.	Bebington	O	X	X
Bean, R.	Rochester	—	O	X
Benn, A.	Bristol SE	O	—	O
Bennett, A.	Stockport N	O	O	O
Bidwell, S.	Southall	O	O	O
Bishop, E.	Newark	X	X	X
Blenkinsop, A.	S Shields	X	X	—
Broadman, H.	Leigh	X	—	X
Booth, A.	Barrow	O	—	O
Boothroyd, Miss B.	W Bromwich W	X	X	X
Bottomley, A.	Middlesbrough	X	X	O
Boyden, J.	Bishop Auckland	X	X	—
Bradley, T.	Leicester E	X	X	X
Bray, J.	Motherwell	X	X	O
Broughton, Sir A.	Batley	X	—	—
Brown, H.	Glasgow Provan	X	X	X
Brown, R.	Newcastle W	X	X	X
Brown, R.	Hackney S	X	X	X
Buchan, N.	Renfrew W	O	—	O
Buchanan, R.	Glasgow S'burn	X	X	—
Butler, Mrs J.	Wood Green	O	—	O
Callaghan, J.	Cardiff SE	X	X	X

TABLE 2 — *Cont.*

LAB MP	Constituency	Europe R	DE	PR
Callaghan, J.	Middleton	O	—	O
Campbell, I.	Dunbart'shire W	O	—	—
Canavan, D.	Stirlingshire W	—	O	O
Cant, R.	Stoke C	X	X	X
Carmichael, N.	Glasgow K'grove	O	O	O
Carter, R.	B'ham Northfield	X	X	X
Carter-Jones, L.	Eccles	O	O	O
Cartwright, J.	Woolwich E	X	X	X
Castle, Mrs B.	Blackburn	O	O	O
Clemitson, J.	Luton E	O	—	O
Cocks, M.	Bristol S	O	X	X
Coben, S.	Leeds SE	X	X	—
Coleman, D.	Neath	X	X	X
Colquhoun, Ms M.	Northampton N	O	O	X
Concannon, D.	Mansfield	—	X	X
Conlan, B.	Gateshead E	—	—	X
Cook, R.	Edinburgh C	O	O	X
Corbett, R.	Hemel Hempstead	O	X	X
Cowans, H.	Newcastle C	N	—	O
Cox, T.	Tooting	O	—	O
Cragen, J.	Glasgow M'hill	X	—	X
Crawshaw, R.	Liverpool Toxteth	X	X	X
Cronin, J.	Loughborough	X	X	X
Crowther, S.	Rotherham	N	O	X
Cryer, R.	Keighley	O	—	O
Cunningham, G.	Islington S	O	O	O
Cunningham, J.	Whitehaven	X	X	—
Dalyell, T.	West Lothian	—	X	—
Davidson, A.	Accrington	—	—	X
Davies, B.	Enfield N	O	O	O
Davies, D.	Llanelli	O	—	X
Davies I.	Gower	X	X	X
Dacis, S.C.	Hackney C	O	—	X
Deakins, E.	Walthamstow	—	—	O
Dean, J.	Leeds W	O	O	—
De Freitas, G.	Kettering	X	X	X
Dell, E.	Birkenhead	X	X	X
Dempsey, J.	Coatbridge	O	X	O
Dewar, D.	Garscadden	N	N	N
Doig, P.	Dundee W	X	X	O
Dormand, J.	Easington	—	X	O
Douglas-Mann, B.	Mitcham	O	X	X

TABLE 2 — *Cont.*

LAB MP	Constituency	Europe R	DE	PR
Duffy, P.	Sheffield A'cliffe	X	X	X
Dunn, J.	L'pool Kirkdale	X	X	—
Dunnett, J.	Nottingham E	X	X	X
Dunwoody, Mrs G.	Crewe	O	O	O
Eadie, A.	Midlothian	O	—	O
Edge, G.	Aldridge	O	—	X
Edwards, R.	Wolverhampton SE	—	—	—
Ellis, J.	Brigg	O	O	O
Ellis, T.	Wrexham	X	X	X
English, M.	Nottingham W	O	X	O
Ennals, D.	Norwich N	X	X	X
Evans, A.	Caerphilly	O	—	O
Evans, I.	Aberdare	O	O	O
Evans, J.	Newton	O	—	O
Ewing, H.	Stirling	O	—	X
Faulds, A.	Warley W	—	X	X
Fernyhough, E.	Jarrow	O	O	O
Fitch, A.	Wigan	X	X	X
Flannery, M.	Sheffield H'b'gh	O	O	O
Fletcher, E.	Darlington	O	O	O
Fletcher, R.	Ilkeston	—	—	—
Foot, M.	Ebbw Vale	O	—	X
Ford, B.	Bradford N	X	X	—
Forrester, J.	Stoke N	O	O	O
Fowler, G.	Wrekin	X	X	X
Fraser, J.	Norwood	O	—	X
Freeson, R.	Brent E	O	—	O
Galpern, Sir M.	Glasgow S'leson	S	S	S
Garrett, J.	Norwich S	X	—	O
Garrett, E.	Wallsend	O	O	O
George, B.	Walsall N	O	X	X
Gilbert, J.	Dudley E	O	—	X
Ginsburg	Dewsbury	X	X	X
Golding, J.	Newcastle-u-L'me	X	X	X
Gould, B.	Southampton T'st	O	O	O
Gourlay, H.	Kirkcaldy	O	X	X
Graham, E.	Edmonton	X	X	X
Grant, G.	Morpeth	X	—	O
Grant, J.	Islington C	X	X	X
Grocott, B.	Lichfield	—	—	O
Hamilton, J.	Bothwell	O	—	X
Hamilton, W.	Fife C	X	X	X

TABLE 2 — *Cont.*

LAB MP	Constituency	R	Europe DE	PR
Hardy, P.	Rother Valley	O	—	O
Harper, J.	Pontefract	X	X	X
Harrison, W.	Wakefield	O	X	X
Hare, Mrs J.	Lanark	O	—	—
Hattersley, R.	B'ham S'brook	X	X	X
Hayman, Mrs H.	Welwyn	X	—	O
Healey, D.	Leeds E	X	X	X
Heffer, E.	Liverpool Walton	O	O	O
Hooley, F.	Sheffield Heeley	O	O	X
Horam, J.	Gateshead W	X	X	X
Howell, D.	B'ham S Heath	X	X	X
Hoyle, D.	Nelson	O	O	O
Huckfield, L.	Nuneaton	O	—	O
Hughes, C.	Anglesey	X	X	X
Hughes, M.	Durham	O	—	—
Hughes, R.	Aberdeen N	O	X	O
Hughes, R.	Newport	O	O	O
Hunter, A.	Dunfermline	O	O	O
Irvine, Sir A.	Liverpool E Hill	O	—	—
Irving, S.	Dartford	X	—	X
Jackson, C.	Brighouse	X	X	X
Jackson, Miss M.	Lincoln	O	—	O
Janner, G.	Leicester W	X	X	O
Jay, D.	Battersea N	O	O	O
Jeger, Mrs L.	Holborn	—	O	O
Jenkins, H.	Putney	O	O	O
John, B.	Pontypridd	O	X	X
Johnson, J.	Hull W	X	X	X
Johnson, W.	Derby S	X	X	X
Jones, A.	Rhondda	O	X	—
Jones, B.	Flint E	X	X	X
Jones, D.	Burnley	X	X	X
Judd, F.	Portsmouth N	O	X	X
Kaufman, G.	Manchester A'wick	O	X	X
Kelley, R.	Don Valley	O	O	—
Kerr, R.	Feltham	O	O	O
Kilroy-Silk, R.	Ormskirk	O	O	O
Kinnock, N.	Bedwellty	—	O	—
Lambrie, D.	Ayrshire C	O	O	X
Lamborn, H.	Peckham	X	X	X
Lamond, J.	Oldham E	O	—	O
Latham, A.	Paddington	O	O	O

TABLE 2 — *Cont.*

LAB MP	Constituency	R	*Europe* DE	PR
Leadbitter, E.	Hartlepool	O	O	—
Lee, J.	B'ham H'dsworth	—	O	O
Lestor, Miss J.	Eton	O	O	O
Lever, H.	Manchester C	X	X	X
Lewis, A.	Newham NW	O	O	O
Lewis, R.	Carlisle	O	—	O
Litterick, T.	B'ham Selly Oak	O	O	O
Lomas, K.	Huddersfield W	X	X	O
Loyden, E.	Liverpool G'ston	O	O	O
Luard, E.	Oxford	X	X	X
Lyon, A.	York	X	X	O
Lyons, E.	Bradford W	X	X	X
Mabon, Dr D	Greenock	X	X	X
McCartney, H.	Dunbarton C	—	O	O
McDonald, Dr O	Thurrock	N	—	O
McElhone, F.	Glasgow Q Park	O	—	X
MacFarquhar, R.	Belper	X	X	X
McGuire, M.	Ince	X	—	X
Mackenzie, G.	Rutherglen	X	X	X
Mackintosh, J.	Berwick & E Lothian	X	X	X
Maclennan, R.	Caithness	X	X	X
McMillan, T.	Glasgow C	O	O	O
McNamara, K.	Hull C	O	—	—
Madden, M.	Sowerby	O	O	O
Magee, B.	Leyton	X	X	X
Mahon, S.	Bootle	X	X	—
Mallalieu, J.	Huddersfield	X	X	X
Marks, K.	Manchester Gorton	X	X	X
Marshall, E.	Goole	O	X	X
Marshall, J.	Leicester S	—	—	O
Mason, R.	Barnsley	X	—	X
Maynard, Miss J.	Sheffield B'side	O	O	O
Meacher, M.	Oldham W	O	—	O
Mellish, R.	Bermondsey	X	X	O
Mikardo, I.	Bethnal Green	O	O	O
Milan, B.	Glasgow C'gton	X	—	X
Miller, Dr M.	E Kilbride	O	—	—
Mitchell, A.	Grimsby	N	O	—
Mitchell, R.	Southampton It'n	X	X	—
Molloy, W.	Ealing N	O	—	O
Moonman, E.	Basildon	X	—	—
Morris, A.	Manchester Wyth	—	—	O

TABLE 2 — *Cont.*

LAB MP	Constituency	R	Europe DE	PR
Morris, C.	Manchester O'shaw	O	—	—
Morris, J.	Aberavon	X	X	X
Moyle, R.	Lewisham E	—	—	—
Mulley, F.	Sheffield Park	—	X	X
Murray, R.K.	Leith	—	—	X
Newens, S.	Harlow	O	O	O
Noble, M.	Rossendale	O	—	O
Oakes, G.	Widnes	X	X	X
Ogden, E.	Liverpool W Derby	X	X	X
O'Halloran, M.	Islington N	O	X	O
Orbach, M.	Stockport S	O	—	O
Orme, S.	Salford W	O	—	O
Ovenden, J.	Gravesend	O	O	X
Owen, Dr D.	Plymouth D'port	X	—	X
Padley, W.	Ogmore	X	X	—
Palmer, A.	Bristol NE	X	—	X
Park, G.	Coventry NE	—	—	—
Parker, J.	Dagenham	X	X	X
Parry, R.	L'pool Scotland	—	—	—
Pavitt, L.	Brent S	O	O	O
Pendry, T.	Stalybridge	O	—	O
Perry, E.	Battersea S	X	—	X
Phipps, Dr C.	Dudley W	X	—	X
Prescott, J.	Hull E	O	—	O
Price, C.	Lewisham W	O	O	O
Price, W.	Rugby	X	X	X
Radice, G.	Chester-le-Street	X	X	X
Rees, M.	Leeds S	X	X	X
Richardson, Miss J.	Barking	O	O	O
Roberts, A.	Normanton	X	—	O
Roberts, G.	Cannock	O	O	O
Robinson, G.	Coventry NW	N	O	O
Roderick, C.	Brecon	O	—	O
Rodgers, G.	Chorley	O	O	O
Rodgers, W.	Stockton	X	X	X
Rooker, J.	B'ham Perry Barr	X	X	X
Roper, J.	Farnworth	X	X	X
Rose, P.	Manchester B'ckley	X	X	X
Ross, W.	Kilmarnock	O	—	X
Rowlands, E.	Merthyr	X	X	—
Ryman, J.	Blyth	O	—	O
Sandelson, N.	Hayes	X	X	X

TABLE 2 — Cont.

LAB MP	Constituency	R	Europe DE	PR
Sedgemore, B.	Luton W	O	—	O
Selby, H.	Glasgow Govan	O	—	—
Sever, J.	B'ham Ladywood	N	—	X
Shaw, A.	Ilford S	O	O	O
Sheldon, R.	Ashton-u-Lyme	X	X	X
Shore, P.	Stepney	O	—	O
Short, Mrs R.	Wolverhampton NE	O	—	O
Silkin, J.	Deptford	O	—	—
Silkin, S.	Dulwich	X	X	X
Silverman, J.	B'ham Erdington	O	O	X
Skinner, D.	Bolsover	O	O	O
Smith, J.	Lanark N	X	X	X
Snape, P.	W Bromwich E	O	—	X
Spearing, N.	Newham S	O	O	O
Spriggs, L.	St Helens	O	—	O
Stallard, J.	St Pancras N	O	—	X
Stewart, M.	Fulham	X	X	X
Stoddart, D.	Swindon	O	O	O
Stott, R.	Westhoughton	O	X	X
Strang, G.	Edinburgh E	X	—	X
Strauss, G.	Vauxhall	X	X	X
Summerskill, Dr S.	Halifax	X	X	X
Swain, T.	Derbyshire SE	O	—	—
Taylor, Mrs A.	Bolton W	—	—	—
Thomas, J.	Abertillery	X	X	X
Thomas, M.	Newcastle E	X	X	X
Thomas, R.	Bristol NW	O	O	O
Thorne, S.	Preston S	O	O	O
Tuerney, S.	B'ham Yardley	O	—	O
Tilley, J.	Lambeth C	N	N	N
Tinn, J.	Redcar	X	X	—
Tomlinson, J.	Meriden	X	X	X
Tomney, F.	Hammersmith N	X	—	—
Torney, T.	Bradford S	O	O	O
Tuck, R.	Watford	—	—	—
Urwin, T.	Houghton-le-S'ng	O	O	O
Varley, E.	Chesterfield	O	—	X
Wainwright, E.	Dearne Valley	X	—	X
Walker, H.	Doncaster	O	—	X
Walker, T.	Kingswood	—	X	X
Ward, M.	Peterborough	X	X	X
Watkins, D.	Consett	X	X	X

TABLE 2 — *Cont.*

LAB MP	Constituency	R	Europe DE	PR
Watkinson, J.	Glo'stershire W	O	—	X
Weetch, K.	Ipswich	O	—	X
Weitzman, D.	Hackney N	O	X	X
Wellbeloved, J.	Erith	X	—	X
White, F.	Bury & Radcliffe	X	X	X
White, J.	Glasgow Pollok	X	—	—
Whitehead, P.	Derby N	X	X	O
Whitlock, W.	Nottingham N	X	—	X
Willey, F.	Sunderland N	X	X	O
Williams, A.	Swansea W	X	X	X
Williams, A. Lee	Hornchurch	X	X	X
Williams, Mrs S.	Hertford	X	X	X
Williams, Sir T.	Warrington	—	X	—
Wilson, Sir H.	Huyton	X	X	X
Wilson, W.	Coventry SE	O	O	X
Wise, Mrs A	Coventry SW	O	O	O
Woodall, A.	Hemsworth	—	X	X
Woof, R.	Blaydon	O	O	O
Wrigglesworth, I.	Thornaby	X	X	X
Young, D.	Bolton E	—	—	X
CON MP				
Adley, R.	Christchurch	X	—	O
Aitken, J.	Thanet E	X	O	O
Alison, M.	Barkston Ash	—	X	O
Amery, J.	Brighton Pavilion	X	X	O
Arnold, T.	Hazelgrove	X	X	O
Atkins, H.	Spelthorne	X	X	O
Atkinson, D.	Bournemouth E	N	N	O
Awdry, D.	Chippenham	X	X	X
Baker, K.	St Marylebone	X	X	X
Banks, R.	Harrogate	X	—	O
Bell, R.	Beaconsfield	O	O	O
Bennett, Sir F.	Torbay	X	X	—
Bennett, Dr R.	Fareham	X	X	O
Benyon, W.	Buckingham	X	X	X
Berry, A.	Southgate	X	X	O
Biffen, J.	Oswestry	O	O	O
Biggs-Davison, J.	Epping F	X	X	O
Blaker, P.	Blackpool S	X	X	O
Body, R.	Holland	O	O	O

TABLE 2 — *Cont.*

CON MP	Constituency	R	Europe DE	PR
			Europe	
Boscawen, R.	Wells	X	X	O
Bottomley, P.	Woolwich W	N	X	X
Bowden, A.	Brighton Kemp T	X	X	O
Boyson, R.	Brent N	X	X	O
Braine, Sir B.	Essex SE	—	X	O
Brittan, L.	Cleveland	X	X	O
Brocklebank-Fowler, C.	Norfolk NW	—	X	X
Brooke, P.	L'don & Westminster	N	X	X
Brotherton, M.	Louth	X	X	O
Brown, Sir E.	Bath	X	X	O
Bryan, Sir P.	Howden	X	X	O
Buchanan-Smith, A.	Angus N	X	X	X
Buck, A.	Colchester	X	X	O
Budgen, N.	Wolverhampton SW	X	O	O
Bulmer, E.	Kidderminster	X	X	X
Burden, F.	Gillingham	X	X	O
Butler, A.	Bosworth	X	X	O
Carlisle, M.	Runcorn	X	X	X
Chalker, Mrs L.	Wallasey	X	X	X
Channon, P.	Southend W	X	X	O
Churchill, W.	Stretford	X	X	O
Clark, A.	Plymouth Sutton	O	O	O
Clark, W.	Croydon S	X	X	O
Clarke, W.	Rushcliffe	X	X	O
Clegg, W.	Fylde N	X	X	O
Cockcroft, J.	Nantwich	X	X	X
Cooke, R.	Bristol W	X	X	O
Cope, J.	Gloucestershire S	X	X	O
Cormack, P.	SW Staffs	X	O	O
Corrie, J.	Ayr N & Bute	X	—	O
Costain, A.	Folkestone	X	X	O
Critchley, J.	Aldershot	X	X	X
Crouch, D.	Canterbury	X	X	X
Crowder, P.	Ruislip	X	X	O
Davies, J.	Knutsford	X	X	—
Dean, P.	Somerset N	X	X	X
Dodsworth, G.	Herts SW	X	X	X
Douglas-Hamilton, Lord J.	Edinburgh W	X	X	O
Drayson, B.	Skipton	X	X	X
Du Cann, E.	Taunton	—	—	O
Durant, A.	Reading N	X	X	O

TABLE 2 — *Cont.*

CON MP	Constituency	R	Europe DE	PR
Dykes, H.	Harrow E	X	X	X
Eden, Sir J.	Bournemouth W	X	X	O
Edwards, N.	Pembroke	X	X	O
Elliott, Sir W.	Newcastle N	X	—	—
Emery, P.	Honiton	X	—	O
Eyre, R.	B'ham Hall Green	X	X	O
Fairbairn, N.	Kinross	X	X	O
Fairgrieve, R.	Aberdeenshire W	X	X	X
Farr, J.	Harborough	—	—	O
Fell, A.	Yarmouth	X	—	O
Finsberg, G.	Hampstead	X	X	O
Fisher, Sir N.	Surbiton	X	X	X
Fletcher, A.	Edinburgh N	X	X	X
Fketcher-Cooke, C.	Darwen	X	—	O
Fookes, Miss J.	Plymouth Drake	—	X	O
Forman, N.	Carshalton	N	X	O
Fowler, N.	Sutton Coldfield	X	X	O
Fox, M.	Shipley	X	X	O
Fraser, H.	Stafford	X	O	O
Fry, P.	Wellingborough	X	O	O
Galbraith, T.	Glasgow H'head	X	X	O
Gardiner, G.	Reigate	—	X	O
Gardner, E.	S Fylde	X	X	O
Gilmour, Sir I	Amersham	X	X	X
Gilmour, Sir J.	Fife E	X	—	O
Glyn, Dr A.	Windsor	X	X	O
Godber, J.	Grantham	X	X	O
Goodhart, P.	Beckenham	X	X	O
Goodhew, V.	St Albans	X	X	O
Goodlad, A.	Northwich	X	X	X
Gorst, J.	Hendon N	X	X	O
Gow, I.	Eastbourne	X	O	O
Gower, Sir R.	Barry	X	X	X
Grant, J.A.	Harrow C	X	X	—
Gray, H.	Ross & Cromarty	X	X	O
Grieve, P.	Solihull	X	X	O
Griffiths, E.	Bury St E	X	X	O
Grist, I.	Cardiff N	X	X	O
Grylls, M.	Surrey NW	X	X	O
Hall-Davis, A.	Morecambe	X	X	O
Hamilton, M.	Salisbury	X	X	O
Hampson, K.	Ripon	X	X	X

TABLE 2 — *Cont.*

CON MP	Constituency	R	Europe DE	PR
Hannam, J.	Exeter	X	X	O
Harrison, Sir H.	Eye	X	X	—
Harvie Anderson, Ms B.	Renfrew E	X	—	O
Haselhurst, A.	Saffron Walden	N	X	X
Hastings, S.	Mid-Beds	X	X	O
Havers, Sir M.	Wimbledon	X	X	O
Hawkins, P.	Norfolk SW	—	—	O
Hayhoe, B.	Brentford	X	X	X
Heath, E.	Bexley	X	X	X
Heseltine, M.	Henley	X	X	O
Hicks, R.	Bodmin	X	—	—
Higgins, T.	Worthing	X	X	O
Hodgson, R.	Walsall N	N	X	O
Holland, P.	Carlton	X	X	O
Hordern, P.	Horsham	X	X	O
Howe, Sir G.	Surrey E	X	X	O
Howell, D.	Guildford	X	X	O
Howell, R.	Norfolk N	X	X	O
Hunt, D.	Wirral	N	X	X
Hunt, J.	Ravensbourne	—	X	—
Hurd, D.	Mid Oxon	X	X	O
Hutchinson, M.C.	Edinburgh S	O	O	O
Irvine, B.G.	Rye	X	S	S
Irving, C.	Cheltenham	X	X	O
James, D.	Dorset N	X	X	—
Jenkin, P.	Wanstead	X	X	O
Jessel, T.	Twickenham	—	X	O
Johnson Smith, G.	E Grinstead	X	—	X
Jones, A.	Daventry	X	X	O
Jopling, M.	Westmorland	X	X	O
Joseph, Sir K.	Leeds NE	X	X	O
Kaberry, Sir D.	Leeds NW	X	X	O
Kellett-Bowman, Mrs E.	Lancaster	X	X	O
Kershaw, A.	Stroud	X	X	X
Kimball, M.	Gainsborough	X	—	O
King, E.M.	Dorset S	X	X	X
King, T.	Bridgwater	X	X	O
Kitson, Sir T.	Richmond, Yorks	X	—	O
Knight, Mrs J.	B'ham E'gbaston	X	X	O
Knox, D.	Leek	X	X	X
Lamont, N.	Kingston-on-Thames	X	X	O
Langford-Holt, Sir J.	Shrewsbury	X	X	O

TABLE 2 — *Cont.*

CON MP	Constituency	R	Europe DE	PR
Latham, M.	Melton Mowbray	X	X	X
Lawrence, I.	Burton	X	X	O
Lawson, N.	Blaby	X	X	O
Le Marchant, S.	High Peak	X	X	O
Lester, J.	Beeston	X	X	X
Lewis, K.	Rutland	X	X	X
Lloyd, I.	Havant	X	—	X
Loveridge, J.	Upminster	X	X	O
Luce, R.	Shoreham	X	X	—
McAdden, Sir S.	Southend E	—	—	O
McCrindle, R.	Brentwood	X	X	O
MacFarlane, N.	Sutton	X	X	O
MacGregor, J.	Norfolk S	X	X	O
Mackay, A.	B'ham Stechford	N	X	O
Macmillan, M.	Farnham	X	—	O
McNair Wilson, M.	Newbury	X	—	O
McNair Wilson, P.	New Forest	X	X	O
Madel, D.	Beds S	X	X	O
Marshall, M.	Arundel	X	X	O
Marten, N.	Banbury	O	O	O
Mates, M.	Petersfield	X	X	O
Mather, C.	Esher	X	X	O
Maude, A.	Stratford	X	X	—
Maudling, R.	Barnet	X	X	X
Mawby, R.	Totnes	X	X	O
Maxwell-Hyslop, R.	Tiverton	X	O	O
Mayhew, P.	Tunbridge Wells	X	X	X
Meyer, Sir A.	Flint W	X	X	X
Miller, H.	Bromsgrove	X	X	O
Mills, P.	Devon W	X	X	O
Miscampbell, F.	Blackpool N	X	X	X
Mitchell, D.	Basingstoke	X	X	X
Moate, R.	Faversham	O	O	O
Monro, H.	Dumfries	X	X	O
Montgomery, F.	Altrincham	X	X	O
Moore, J.	Croydon C	X	X	O
More, J.	Ludlow	—	—	O
Morgan G.	Denbigh	—	X	O
Morgan-Giles, Rr.-Ad., M.	Winchester	X	—	O
Morris, M.	Northampton S	X	X	—
Morrison, C.	Devizes	X	X	X
Morrison, P.	Chester	X	X	O

Voting Records

TABLE 2 — Cont.

CON MP	Constituency	R	Europe DE	PR
Mudd, D.	Falmouth	–	–	O
Murton, P.	Poole	S	S	S
Neave, A.	Abingdon	X	X	O
Nelson, A.	Chichester	X	–	O
Neubert, M.	Romsford	X	X	O
Newton, A.	Braintree	X	X	X
Normanton, T.	Cheadle	X	X	O
Nott, J.	St Ives	X	X	O
Onslow, C.	Woking	X	X	–
Oppenheim, Mrs. S.	Gloucester	X	X	O
Osborn, J.	Sheffield Hallam	X	X	O
Page, J.	Harrow W	X	–	O
Page, R.G.	Crosby	X	X	O
Page, R.	Workington	N	X	O
Parkinson, C.	S Herts	X	X	O
Pattie, G.	Chertsey	X	X	O
Percival, I.	Southport	X	X	O
Peyton, J.	Yeovil	X	X	–
Pink, R.B.	Portsmouth S	X	X	–
Prentice, R.	Newham NE	X	X	–
Price, D.	Eastleigh	X	X	O
Prior, J.	Lowestoft	X	–	X
Pym, F.	Cambridgeshire	X	X	O
Raison, T.	Aylesbury	X	X	X
Rathbone, T.	Lewes	X	X	X
Rees, P.	Dover	X	X	O
Rees-Davies, W.	Thanet W	X	X	O
Renton, Sir D.	Huntingdon	X	X	O
Renton, T.	Mid-Sussex	X	X	O
Rhodes James, R.	Cambridge	N	X	X
Rhys Williams, Sir B.	Kensington	X	X	X
Ridley, N.	Cirencester	X	X	O
Ridsdale, J.	Harwich	X	X	O
Rifkind, M.	Ed'burgh P'tlands	X	X	X
Rippon, G.	Hexham	X	X	O
Roberts, M.	Cardiff NW	X	X	O
Roberts, W.	Conway	X	X	O
Rodgers, Sir J.	Sevenoaks	X	–	O
Rossi, H.	Hornsey	X	X	O
Rost, P.	Derbyshire SE	X	–	O
Royle, Sir A.	Richmond	X	X	O
Sainsbury, T.	Hove	X	X	–

TABLE 2 — *Cont.*

CON MP	Constituency	R	Europe DE	PR
St John-Stevas, N.	Chelmsford	X	X	—
Scott, N.	Paddington	X	X	X
Scott-Hopkins, J.	Derbyshire W	X	X	O
Shaw, G.	Pudsey	X	X	O
Shaw, M.	Scarborough	X	—	—
Shelton, W.	Streatham	X	X	O
Shepherd, C.	Hereford	X	X	O
Shersby M.	Uxbridge	X	X	O
Silvester, F.	M'chester W'gton	X	X	O
Sims, R.	Chislehurst	X	X	O
Sinclair, Sir G.	Dorking	X	X	X
Skeet, T.	Bedford	X	—	O
Smith, D.	Warwick	X	X	O
Smith, T.	Ashfield	N	X	X
Speed, K.	Ashford	X	X	O
Spence, J.	Thirsk	—	X	O
Spicer, J.	Dorset W	X	X	O
Spicer, M.	Worcs S	X	X	O
Sproat, I.	Aberdeen S	X	X	O
Stainton, K.	Sudbury	X	X	O
Stanbrook, I.	Orpington	X	X	O
Stanley, J.	Tonbridge	X	X	O
Steen, A.	L'pool Wavertree	X	X	O
Stewart, I.	Hitchin	X	X	X
Stokes, J.	Halesowen	X	O	O
Stradling Thomas, J.	Monmouth	X	X	O
Tapsell, P.	Horncastle	X	X	O
Taylor, E.	Glasgow C'cart	O	X	O
Taylor, R.	Croydon NW	X	—	O
Tebbit, N.	Chingford	X	—	O
Temple-Morris, P.	Leominster	X	X	X
Thatcher, Mrs M.	Finchley	X	X	O
Thomas, P.	Hendon S	X	X	O
Townsend, C.	Bexleyheath	—	X	X
Trotter, N.	Tynemouth	—	X	O
Van Straubenzee, W.	Wokingham	X	X	O
Vaughan, Dr G.	Reading S	X	X	O
Viggers, P.	Gosport	X	—	X
Wakeham, J.	Maldon	X	X	O
Walder, D.	Clitheroe	X	X	O
Walker, P.	Worcester	X	X	X
Walker-Smith, Sir D.	Herts E	X	X	O

TABLE 2— *Cont.*

CON MP	Constituency	R	*Europe* *DE*	*PR*
Wall, P.	Haltemprice	X	X	—
Walters, D.	Westbury	X	X	X
Warren, K.	Hastings	—	—	O
Weatherill, B.	Croydon NE	X	X	O
Wells, J.	Maidstone	X	X	O
Whitelaw, W.	Penrith	X	X	O
Wiggin, J.	Weston-s-Mare	X	X	O
Winterton, N.	Macclesfield	X	O	O
Wood, R.	Bridlington	X	X	X
Young, Sir G.	Acton	X	X	X
Younger, G.	Ayr	X	X	X
LIB **MP**				
Beith, A.	Berwick	X	X	X
Freud, C.	Isle of Ely	X	X	X
Grimond, J.	Orkney	X	X	X
Hooson, E.	Montgomery	X	—	X
Howells, G.	Cardigan	X	X	X
Johnston, R.	Inverness	X	X	X
Pardoe, J.	N Cornwall	X	X	X
Penhaligon, D.	Truro	X	X	X
Ross, S.	Isle of Wight	X	X	X
Smith, C.	Rochdale	—	—	X
Steel, D.	Roxburgh	X	X	X
Thorpe, J.	N Devon	X	X	X
Wainwright, R.	Colne Valley	X	X	X
SNP **MP**				
Bain, Mrs M.	Dunbarton E	O	X	—
Crawford, D.	Perth & E P	O	—	—
Ewing, Mrs W.	Moray	O	X	—
Henderson, D.	Aberdeenshire E	O	X	—
McCormick, I.	Argyll	O	X	—
Reid, G.	Stirling E	O	X	—
Stewart, D.	W Isles	O	—	—
Thompson, G.	Galloway	O	X	—
Watt, H.	Banff	O	X	—
Welsh, A.	Angus S	O	X	—
Wilson, G.	Dundee E	O	X	—

TABLE 2 — *Cont.*

UUUC MP	Constituency	R	Europe DE	PR
PC **MP**				
Evans, G.	Carmarthen	O	O	X
Thomas, D.E.	Merioneth	O	O	—
Wigley, D.	Caenarvon	—	O	X
SCOTTISH LAB **MP**				
Robertson, J.	Paisley	O	—	—
Sillars, J.	Ayrshire S	—	—	X
UUUC **MP**				
Bradford, Rev R.	Belfast S	—	O	—
Carson, J.	Belfast N	O	O	O
Craig, W.	Belfast E	—	—	—
Dunlop, J.	Mid-Ulster	O	O	O
Kilfedder, J.	Down N	—	X	—
McCusker, H.	Armagh	O	O	O
Molyneaux, J.	Antrim S	O	O	O
Paisley, I.	Antrim N	—	—	O
Powell, E.	Down S	O	O	O
Ross, W.	Londonderry	O	O	O
ULSTER — OTHERS **MP**				
Fitt, G. (SDLP)	Belfast W	—	X	—
Maguire, F. (Ind)	Fermanagh	—	—	—

Chapter 6

The Debate over Electoral Systems and Representation

Introduction

The passage of the Direct Elections Bill gave rise to one of the most vociferous debates over electoral systems that Britain had seen for over a generation. Although the proponents of proportional representation did not succeed, the debate is certain to continue.

Although Proportional Representation had been one of the planks of the Lib-Lab pact, the parliamentary balance was never in its favour. The inability of Callaghan and some other Ministers to spread their enthusiasm for PR did not result in retaliatory action from the Liberals despite the well-publicised fury of Cyril Smith at the Government's failure to deliver the goods and his subsequent resignation. The situation would not have been favourable for a General Election. Not only because there had been bad opinion polls for both Labour and Liberals, but because the Liberals' policy for forming the pact to safeguard 'the national interest' would, as David Steel pointed out at the time, have lost some of its credibility had they resigned on an essentially European issue. Still, the history of the Regional List system must rank as one of the most curious of any of the soundings on electoral systems in Britain. What appeared to be the greatest weapon the Liberals had had since before the War tuned out to be a paper tiger and the espousal of leading members of the government of an electoral system essentially inimical to its interests (as one of the two major parties) turned out to be something of a bluff which was never called. The consequences of the debate, as opposed to the choice of system proper, has been an even greater determination amongst the Liberals that any further arrangements with parties of government will rely on Proportional Representation, not only for Europe (which will probably happen anyway) but for

Westminster. In the event of another hung Parliament, it is paradoxical to see that it could be that a vote against PR for Europe was in fact a vote for PR at Westminster, given the resolve which was borne out of the Liberals' disillusion.

The Liberal Action Group for Electoral Reform (LAGER) made out a good case for PR, in its most extreme form, the Single Transferable Vote (STV).[1] They drew on reports of the Patijn Convention of 1960[2] and the Twenty-Second Report of the House of Lords Select Committee on the European Communities (75/6 session),[3] both of which gave high priority to the need to represent all shades of political opinion in each member state. They also cited a speech of Mr. Callaghan's from the Debate of 29 March 1976[4] where he referred to the need to ensure 'adequate representation of the constituent parts of the United Kingdom'. However, in this case Callaghan was referring to geographical constituent parts not political ones. Given that the only other party to obviously benefit from a proportional system of election was the SDLP of Northern Ireland whose case had already been accepted as 'special' in its need to be represented, the Liberals were very isolated in their dedication.

Although the Welsh Nationalists were unlikely to gain a seat under the first-past-the-post system without the allocation of well over four seats to Wales, they would have had no extra advantage under a PR system organised Wales-wide either, since the electoral quotient would be 25% and not 10%, their level of vote in the 1974 election. The Scottish Nationalists had the advantage of a vote which was not only high in proportion in Scotland, being 30.4% in October 1974, but also geographically concentrated within the UK as a whole. So, while the first-past-the-post system did not especially favour them for European elections, at the Westminster level it certainly did; consequently they were not strong advocates for change. When Mr. Thorpe asked Reg Underhill, on behalf of the Liberals in Parliament, before the Select Committee, 'Why should one minority be different from any other?'[5] it is not surprising that the reply not only placed different emphasis on the conditions of Northern Ireland and the impossibility of it setting any kind of precedent but concluded with, 'I do not think you can deal with this on fairness . . . Any change in the voting system must have some effect upon the political structure . . . one is dealing with the whole balance of political life in a particular country'.[6] Despite the protestations of Ulster Unionists over the crime of treating Northern Ireland as different to the rest of the United Kingdom, it was the 'political balance' aspect of the status quo which was the real focus of the powerful vested interests lined up against PR.

Despite the obvious advantage PR would have given them, the LAGER members made it clear that it was the faults of the first-past-the-post system which were the real justification for change. Such faults could be broadly classified as those of logic and those of technique. Logically, they suggested that a continuation of the existing system was not relevant to this new election. This was not only because of the mainly proportional systems in use in Europe and the likelihood that an early change in Britain would give them a better bargaining position vis-à-vis the rest when the uniform system was being planned, but also, because there was no government being elected. The destination of the European MPs would remain the European political groups. Therefore all the assumed advantages of strong government resulting from a majority system which tends to produce two large parties alternating in power were not relevant. Equally, the assumed disadvantages of proportional systems were perhaps avoidable for much the same reasons. With fixed-term elections and an embryonic party system in Europe, greater frequency of elections and party fractionalisation which critics have seen as the result of PR[7] were not such strong indictments as they could have been in a national context.

Technically, the landslide results from small swings of opinion in huge first-past-the-post constituencies for European elections suggest that while PR seemed more palatable at the European level the old system could be seen as less so. With each European election likely to fall some time mid-term of a British Government, and with the unpopularity which this usually produces, a delegation of European MPs elected by the traditional method could well be diammetrically opposed to the politics and policy of the Government in power. With only a handful of seats likely to change hands in elections in the European states using PR, the British swing could determine to a great extent the whole of the political balance in the European Parliament.

Of the types of Proportional Representation available,

LAGER dismissed a mixed system of voting. Here additional members without constituencies would be added to those who had won seats, in order to produce a fairer balance of seats and votes without losing the 'geographical' element of an election. This was unacceptable to them because not only would it still leave them underrepresented (with only 12 seats whereas a proportional system which was more rigorous would give them 14), but also it would mean even larger, more unmanageable constituencies than the true majority system. Neither the German list system nor the true Additional Member system would give a voter an individual choice of candidates — another ideal of the Liberals.

The Single Transferable Vote (STV) on the other hand, was seen as the only system which would guarantee fair representation for the parties, while retaining a choice of individual candidates and being suitable for broad geographical divisions if desired. Pointing to the Irish experience of STV, they showed a relationship between high turnout and high proportions of votes being effective in the election of representatives. Whereas the majority system constituencies with large built-in majorities effectively waste those votes which exceed the level required to win the seat from the nearest opponent, STV not only makes these votes effective in the elections of candidates through transfer, but also allows voters to express a preference between individual candidates and these are also effective in the eventual selection of members. Fears that the first round of Direct Elections would produce a low poll were widespread not only in Britain but in Europe as a whole. While the European Parliament thought that money for publicity would avert this, the Labour Party thought that making them coincident with national elections would help despite reservations as to the practicality of holding more than one election at a time.[8] However, the Liberals felt that the choice of the right electoral system was the only solution to this and most of the other problems of the elections.

Community representation under STV would suffer since it requires multi-member constituencies with as many as 5 million voters each. This problem was thought to be outweighed by the fact that the existing levels of involvement of the 'community' with their MPs have been shown to leave a lot to be desired, with less than one fifth of voters ever having written or spoken to their MP and only just over half knowing their MP's name.[9] So the assumed advantages of close involvement at the local level in the political process were to be replaced by a better involvement in the electoral process. Unlike the practice of STV in Holland where national party lists are used, the Regional List system (which was the only form of Proportional Representation produced in the Bill) would have had a set of regional divisions which would be voted on at the same time as the scheme itself was approved. This is a method where a single vote would be placed against a named candidate from a party list and the seats would be distributed according to both party and candidate popularity. It is interesting that the use of the economic planning regions as the basis of the schedule meant that the system did have the advantage of sending representatives from areas with specific agricultural and industrial characteristics and different policies relevant to industrial and other incentives. In terms of European policies likely to have a regional impact, such divisions would have been logical when compared to the lack of administrative or other functions in the proposed European constituencies for the traditional method.

The First-Past-the-Post System

The problems in adapting the first-past-the-post system to European elections fall mainly into four categories. Firstly, there was the problem of using existing Boundary Commissions machinery, the production of a draft schedule and the collection and response to submissions resulting from it. In view of the tight timetable and the 'necessity for early action' outlined in the House of Commons Select Committee's Third Report[10] many observers, political and academic alike felt that it would be much quicker if either the use of Boundary Commissions was dispensed with or an electoral system which did not require such complex divisions of space (such as the Regional List) was used. While the first-past-the-post system was seen to be a *fait accompli* by the end of 1977 the former possibility was tried by John Roper MP who put down an amendment which included a complete schedule of constituencies with the intention of speeding up the system without avoiding democratic control. This was however, lost by the middle of December 1977 because of the restrictions on debate made by the guillotine motion and it was not possible to avoid the complexities of the system

The First-Past-the-Post System

designed for Westminster.

The second difficulty of the first-past-the-post system was pointed out by Ian Gow MP in a parliamentary speech,

> It is a curious but well tried anomaly that the lower down the scale of the administration, the greater is the degree of representation . . . That means that the representation of an elector in this country is in inverse proportion to the assumed importance and power of the layer of government that we envisage . . . a still smaller representation . . . implies a superior authority at the new Assembly (to that of Westminster).[11]

This theoretical problem was translated into rather more concrete terms by Austin Mitchell MP in the *Guardian* (11/9/78), 'Indeed the day is soon coming when the Euro MPs who go to an assembly with neither role nor function (and not even just raison d'etre in my view) will be better staffed, served, and equipped to do their non-job than we are'. So a combination of larger constituencies, staffs and salaries was of considerable concern, not because in themselves it meant any real threat to Parliament but because, to a British mind, these characteristics of the European Parliamentarians represented an enlargement rather than a reduction in their cudos as compared with Westminster, it therefore seemed logical to suggest that their power would be bound to adapt to the level of their status. The alternative view would be that this has merely shown up how underpaid our MPs are in Britain and it is more likely that they will achieve pay parity than that the European Parliament will somehow achieve power parity.

Thirdly, there has been disagreement as to how the constituencies should be drawn. Two options existed, either drawing the new constituencies around existing local or national divisions or an entirely new schedule. The latter was quickly rejected as requiring too much work and producing areas for which the electorate would have no precedent and hence no attachment. In favour of local government boundaries being used as the basis was the fact that there is already a programme for altering the constituencies at the Westminster level to conform to them by 1980 and it would therefore seem logical to have the European Constituencies drawn in anticipation of this. In favour of Westminster constituencies as the basis was the greater ease of drawing the new map from fewer original units since it would vastly reduce the number of alternative possible outcomes. The latter system had the support of the two major parties who considered it would ease party organisation, allowing the use of existing constituency parties as the basis for candidate selection, and would aid in maintaining links between the European and National Parliaments with a European MP being able to consult between 6 and 13 Westminster MPs from his own constituency. In the end it would seem that the parties and Westminster were supreme over the interests of the longer term, which was in doubt anyway since no one can predict when the 'uniform system' will be implemented.

The technicalities of amalgamating Westminster constituencies to produce 81 areas with no more or less than 10% of the national average electorate and showing some respect for county boundaries were not in themselves immense. While the new scale of boundaries meant that any possibility of a 'gerrymander' was unlikely not only because of the reputation of objectivity which the Boundary Commissions have earned but also since any foul play would loom between 6 and 13 times larger than it would at Westminster. This increase in scale did make it more difficult to be fair to all the parties and for this reason the worst case, politically (Northern Ireland), was selected for another system.

TABLE 3
WESTMINSTER QUOTAS FOR UNITED KINGDOM
REGIONS — 1976 FIGURES

	Electorate	Westminster Quota
England	33,756,674	65,419
Scotland	3,733,357	52,592
Wales	2,032,792	56,406
Northern Ireland	1,042,797	86,895

While constituencies which easily conformed to county boundaries were on the whole feasible in the rural areas, the urbanised areas from London to Manchester and the Central valley of Scotland were not so easy to determine with the same rationale. This was shown by the provisional Report of the Boundary Commission and John Roper's schedule. One further problem was the inequity of electorate size in the

Westminster constituencies which had developed over time in an ad hoc manner in the case of Scotland and Wales, and more recently in the case of Northern Ireland, with the dismantling of Stormont. (This can be seen from Table 4.) England's urban areas, especially the inner cities, having experienced continual large scale shifts in population also show varying levels of electorates throughout.

The added problems of drawing up the schedule were the requirements of the Scottish, Welsh and Greater London Boundaries, all of which had to be respected, and all of which created difficulties. In the case of each of the boundaries a map of the October 1974 election[12] shows that, in terms of contemporary voting allegiances, the boundaries were not political ones, given the similarity of voting patterns immediately adjacent to the boundaries on both sides. In London this has produced some curious results, such as the inclusion of Chipping Barnet and Brent South or Kingston and Vauxhall in the same constituencies. There were, however, obvious reasons why these boundaries were kept and the curiosity of some of the resulting areas naturally ensues when adapting from a Westminster system to an entirely different scale of operation, and this is reflected in areas not affected by these boundaries, as in Birmingham South and Midlands Central.

The fourth difficulty has been the lack of consensus as to what effect the first-past-the-post system's use would have upon the second round, or, at least, the first round by a 'common system' and the negotiations leading up to it. As has been shown, each available system was supported by its advocates on the grounds that it would be quick to introduce. Every critic suggested the opposite. Equally, each system was endowed with the possibility of a better bargaining position vis-a-vis the 'common system' if it was chosen. It will be possible to evaluate these claims after the event but it already appears that the Boundary Commissions will have taken at least nine months in preparing their final Report. As comments from Europe are already expressing signs of doubt as to whether 1983 will really see a common system, it could be that 500,000 constituencies will be with us for a while yet. An objective assessment cannot escape concluding that the decision owed more to vested interests than to logic and it could be that this new election could have provided an opportunity for a useful and effective review of the best options on a less interested basis than actually occured.

Seat Allocations Within the UK, Within the Small States, and in the EEC

As the balance of the parties in Westminster would suggest, the allocation of seats within the UK was an issue which loomed very large in some quarters and was almost insignificant in others. Whatever the politicians may have thought, it is clear that the number of options in most of the areas involved was not very great. Despite the agreement of most of the parties that the allocation should be as proportional as possible even this was not possible in some areas. Again, Northern Ireland was to prove a special case with even the Liberals accepting that a proportional solution to the allocation of seats would not work given that the two seats which should have been allocated if population were the only consideration would have meant either one seat each for the UUUC and the SDLP or both seats going to the UUUC. Neither solution would be remotely acceptable. Because of this, if nothing else, the ideals of PR would have had to be modified in order to come to terms with the realities of Britain's sub-national areas and their special requirements. These realities can be listed as follows, Northern Ireland at least 3 seats, Wales 4-5, Scotland 7-9 seats, and Greater London 9-12 seats. As can be seen from Figure 5 the difference of one seat in areas of low population can make an enormous difference to the number of electors per seat.

Proposals sent to the Select Committee were essentially unenthusiastic on this subject. There were specific regional requests from the Highland Regional Council and the Cornish Nationalist Party for each to have a single seat for the purpose of homogeneity of culture and economy either as a vehicle of nationalism or as a bargaining tool for the European Regional Fund. In this situation it can be seen that some of the problems which could have been solved with a regional list system were translated into a problem of seat allocation under the traditional system but in these two cases neither system would have satisfied their demands given their low populations.[13] In areas of sparse population with regional and identity interests the main vehicles were the Nationalist parties whose case was presented at the level of the small states. See Figure 6 for the possible range of seats in the UK.

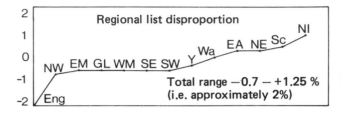

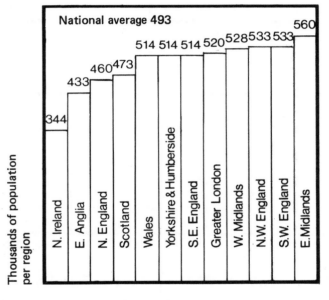

Figure 5 Regional list disproportion.

The small states of Europe are a mixture of a) peripheral areas with predominantly primary industries and ailing employment prospects, most of which have not yet acquired national status, b) wealthier states of industry, such as Luxembourg, and c) highly sophisticated agricultural and industrial economies such as Belgium and Denmark; but they are united in one sense — that of the reality, for the independent states, and the hope, for the sub-national regions, of overrepresentation in the Assembly. Given the inevitable overrepresentation of Ulster, and the problem raised by the coincidence of Scotland's Devolution

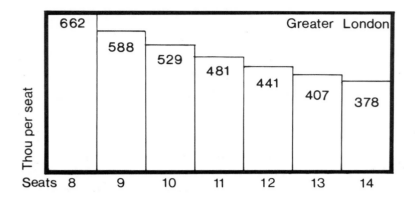

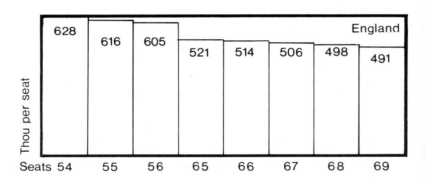

Figure 6 Possible ranges of seats for constituent parts of the UK with the resulting electoral quotas.

Seat Allocations

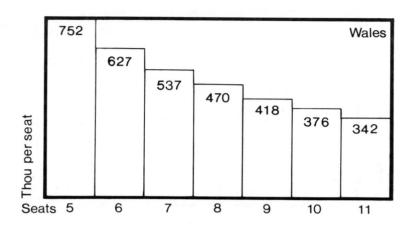

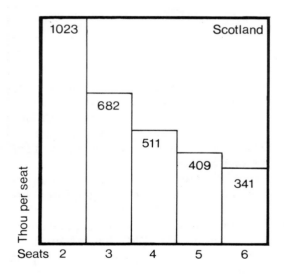

Figure 6 (cont.)

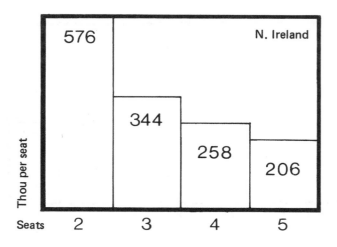

Figure 6 (cont.)

legislation it was clear that Britain's internal allocation of seats would raise a large number of questions in Nationalist lobbies. However, the leeway which was allowed for coping with this within the United Kingdom was immeasureably smaller than it had been within the EEC as a whole. In France where forces for the independence of some regions were also gaining momentum, the situation has been averted, after a lot of hard thinking in Government circles, by a national list for the election. This ensured that every French European MP will be 'French' rather than 'Breton', 'Languedoc', or, 'Corsican'. The continued over-representation of smaller states in the EEC has meant that all sub nationalities have had a further premium put upon independence, given the immediate doubling or trebling of their representation which this would produce.

If this is coupled with the increasing tendency in the Scottish Nationalist Party to aim at high level personnel being sent to Brussels offices, putting the 'Scottish' case in a new forum where there are many potential allies and a growing Regional Fund, one can see that the role which Europe could play in what has formerly been a domestic issue may become more important, and that of London less so. As Mrs. Ewing pointed out during a press conference in Glasgow in 1978, 'Our fellow Europeans are now aware of the very real discontent in Scotland over deals done by the British Government on such vital issues as steel, fishing, energy, and agriculture'. Rather than falling into either of the pro- or anti-Federalist lobbies in Europe and avoiding the European Political groupings, the Scottish Nationalists may well be seeking to use Europe as a way of bypassing London, after establishing a power base in the new Assembly in Edinburgh.

The combination of Direct Elections and Devolution legislation has not produced the prospect of complete harmony, however. One difficulty was pointed out by the 'Scotland in Europe' group, 'We fully realise that moves towards Direct Elections in 1978 could present many problems for Scotland, due to the fact that we are to have elections for the Scottish Regions that year and therefore Scottish electors might be faced with a diet of too many elections in too short a period, especially if a Scottish Assembly is created.'[14] In fact the situation may be worse than this with the likelihood of an early General Election in 1979, the local elections in May and the Direct Elections in June with the Assembly's elections having been promised in March, and the campaign having started even earlier. This will mean four elections in six months with the European Elections coming last, so the problems of a low poll, probable in most of Europe, will be almost inevitable in Scotland and Wales. The second difficulty in the Devolution legislation is whether the divisions between 'home' and 'foreign' policy which are made are realistic in relation to the workings of the EEC today. It would appear from the work of T. S. Bates[15] that whereas the strategy of European policy will stay at Westminster the tactics of EEC policy implementation will move to Edinburgh and thus there will be potential for a direct Europe/Scotland link.

The problem of balancing the representation of Scotland and Denmark has been a very real one and it is yet to be solved. Despite the ingenuity of some of the proposals put forward such as that of the Liberal Peer, Lord Gladwyn, of two different types of European MPs, the 'real' and the 'substitute', with under-representation of one type being made up with the other,[16] it is difficult to avoid perpetuation of what Scottish people would

105

see as second class representation of Scotland or Britain's other regional minorities. This will prolong an attack which would be well founded if one believed in either the right of Scotland to independence or the inequity of weighted seat allocations in Europe. As 'Scotland in Europe' suggests, if Scotland has as few as half the number of seats of Denmark, 'then the question of Scottish seats will rumble on as a political issue for years and years'.[17]

The allocation of seats between Member States in the EEC as a whole has received considerable attention in Europe since the first real move towards Direct Elections in 1960. To some extent seat allocation served the same function in the debate as some technical issues did in Britain, acting as a focus of anti-Direct Election supporters and becoming all the more intractable as a result. At one level, it is easy to see why the technicalities of representing the two Europe's — the large states and the small — would be highly complex in the context of a Parliament expected to be between half and two thirds the size of most of the National parliaments involved.

However, as with all institutional changes in the EEC, the matter was really inextricably bound up with the question of sovereignty. The situation of Luxembourg, while apparently the most difficult became accepted as being so amonalous that special allowances for her size and sovereignty would have to be made. The fact that she already had 6 seats in the non-elected Parliament and that however small her population she considered it right that all shades of political opinion should be represented in rough proportion, meant that any hope of seat allocations being truly proportional was more or less doomed from the start. However, the situation was worsened by the fact that Luxembourg was never thought to be a special case in the sense that she should be the only member state to enjoy considerable overrepresentation. Belgium and Holland, and, more recently, Denmark and Ireland (the other components of the small states bloc) were also considered to be worthy of similar privileges. This was thought to be part of a long standing pattern in European institutions. Instruments such as the veto in the Council of Ministers and other technical barriers helped to ensure that nationality was more important than size or strength so that the interests of the larger powers could not swamp those of the others. It was realised that moves to make the system in Europe less dependent upon the maintainance of

Seat Allocations

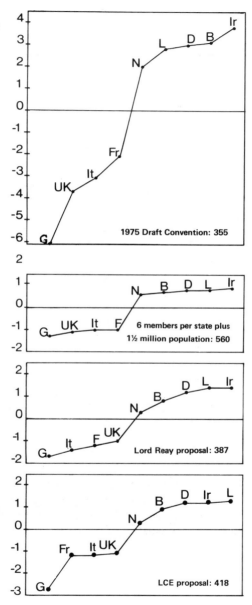

Figure 7 Proposals for EEC seat allocations.

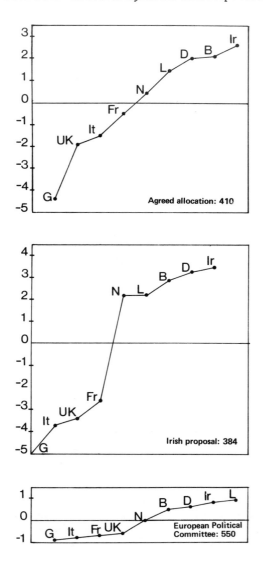

Figure 7 (Cont.)

Seat Allocations

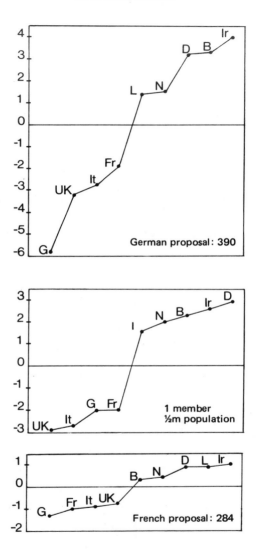

Figure 7 (Cont.)

TABLE 4
PROPOSED EEC SEAT ALLOCATIONS

		Pre-election Allocation (1)	1960 Draft Convention Committee (2)	EP Political Committee (3)	French Proposal (4)	Irish Proposal (5)	Lord Reay Proposal (6)	LCE Proposal (7)	German Proposal (8)	1 member/ ½m. popn. (9)	6 members + 1/½m. popn. (10)	1975 Draft Convention (11)	Agreed Allocation (12)
GERMANY	seats	36	108 as for col. (1)	128	65	74	87	94	72	123	129	71	81
	seats/ electorate gap %	−6.1		−0.9	−1.3	−5.0	−1.7	−2.7	−5.7	NIL	−1.3	−2.0	−4.4
UK	seats	36	108	116	59	70	80	86	72	111	117	67	81
	seats/ electorate gap %	−3.7		−0.6	−0.1	−3.4	−1.0	−1.1	−3.2	NIL	−1.1	−2.9	−1.9
ITALY	seats	36	108	113	58	69	77	84	72	108	114	66	81
	seats/ electorate gap %	−3.1		−0.8	−0.9	−3.7	−1.4	−1.2	−2.8	NIL	−1.0	−2.7	−1.5
FRANCE	seats	36	108	108	55	68	74	80	72	103	109	65	81
	seats/ electorate gap %	−2.1		−0.7	−1.0	−2.6	−1.2	−1.2	−1.9	NIL	−1.0	−2.0	−0.5
NETHERLANDS	seats	14	42	31	17	30	23	25	28	26	32	27	25
	seats/ electorate gap %	2.0		0.0	0.4	2.2	0.3	0.3	1.5	NIL	0.6	2.0	0.4
BELGIUM	seats	14	42	24	13	26	18	20	28	19	25	23	24
	seats/ electorate gap %	3.1		0.5	0.3	2.9	0.8	0.9	3.3	NIL	0.7	2.3	2.1
DENMARK	seats	10	30	14	8	20	12	13	20	10	16	17	16
	seats/ electorate gap %	3.0		0.6	0.9	3.3	1.2	1.2	3.2	NIL	0.8	2.9	2.0
IRELAND	seats	10	30	10	6	18	10	10	20	6	12	13	15
	seats/ electorate gap %	3.8		0.7	1.0	3.5	1.4	1.2	4.0	NIL	0.9	2.6	2.6
LUXEMBOURG	seats	6	18	6	3	9	6	6	6	1	6	6	6
	seats/ electorate gap %	2.8		0.9	0.9	2.2	1.4	1.3	1.4	NIL	0.8	1.6	1.4
TOTAL SEATS EP		198	594	550	284	384	387	418	390	506	560	355	410
Range of seats/ electorate gap %		9.9	9.9	1.8	2.3	8.5	3.1	4.0	9.7	NIL	2.1	5.8	7.0

national sovereignty, for example by majority voting in the Council of Ministers, would rely upon an equal strengthening of safeguard measures and for this the role of Direct Elections could be a very important one.

While this has been the basic idea behind most of the proposed seat allocations (see Table 5 and Figure 7), it was not one which appealed overmuch to the French, who saw the protection of the sovereignty of the smaller states as an automatic reduction in their own. The arguments they put forward were of varying starting points but they invariably lead to the same conclusion — no national weighting in seat allocations. This can be shown in two examples, firstly, Mr. Habib-Deloncle's speech to the European Assembly in March 1969:

When it comes to universal suffrage I notice, to take the case of France and Luxembourg as examples, that the population ratio is not 1 to 6 but 1 to 150 . . . But we could put Luxembourg as a class apart, as a product of history, and take the Benelux group as a whole. This comprises about 23 million people, as compared with 59 in Federal Germany, 53 in Italy and 50 million in France. Benelux now has 34 representatives whereas each of the other three has 36. Now the French would not put up with being worth half a Belgian, Dutch or Luxembourg elector . . . All the principles of the 1789 Revolution, all the principles that lead to the introduction of universal suffrage are opposed to this iniquity.[18]

and secondly, in January 1975, the speech of Mr. De La Malene speaking on behalf of the European Progressive Democrats,

It seems to us impossible to aspire to one thing and its opposite at one and the same time. If we are trying to acquire legitimacy and representativeness, if we want to have more authority in our decision-making, we cannot adopt a system of national weighting . . . No one is more concerned than we are about defending the interests of the small . . . But we could point out to all the representatives of the smaller states that election of the European Parliament by universal suffrage is not the way to defend their interests.[19]

As can be seen from the extension of the 1960 Draft Convention allocation for the enlarged Community and the extension of the allocation which existed before enlargement, neither of the established distributions would have been appropriate since the first would produce too large an Assembly and the second too small an Assembly. So, while the situation required a new approach to the problem, the persistence of French opposition to weighting and the committment of the Germans and the small states to continue weighting even at the existing high level,

TABLE 5
PRE-ENLARGEMENT SEAT ALLOCATIONS

	Nos. of Seats	% seats	000s popn. *	% popn.	seat/ popn. gap
Belgium	14	9.85	9.943	5.27	+4.58
France	36	25.36	50,788	26.89	−1.53
Germany	36	25.36	60,540	32.06	−6.70
Italy	36	25.36	53,920	28.55	−3.19
Luxembourg	6	4.22	345	0.18	+4.04
Netherlands	14	9.85	13,309	7.05	+2.80

* 1960 figures

meant that it was going to be difficult to produce an acceptable solution. One useful factor was the fact that of the large states, France was the smallest and hence likely to receive favourable treatment compared with Germany, for example, if all the large states had the same number of seats. As can be seen from the eventual solution, there was a change of heart, in favour of a reduction in weighting, between the 1975 Draft Convention and the eventually decided allocation with the introduction of equal numbers of seats for all the large states — a well balanced compromise.

British views on seat allocations range from the impractical solutions of the Labour Common Market Safeguards Committee who proposed no increase in the number of seats and that of Enoch Powell who recommended a British delegation roughly half the size of Westminster (which would produce an overall Assembly of about 1,500 members) to those of the majority of commentators, who preferred something between 200 and 400 seats, with Britain having 70-85 members. By these criteria, at least, the eventual solution was very much in line with British opinion as a whole although the continued weighting will not ease internal allocations in the UK. The SNP gave a very sophisticated series of suggestions to the House of Commons Select Committee recommending a total Assembly of 425 members, based on a formula of 3 seats per member plus one per 650,000 population. This would result in 5.69 plus 3 seats for Scotland making 8.69, if it was treated as a nation state and 3 plus 3 seats totalling 6 for Wales, under the same conditions. In fact as Scotland will have 8 seats under an interal allocation their solution is one which is aimed at seat parity with the smaller states not through an increase in their own allocation to unreasonable levels, as the members of Plaid Cymru would have done, but through the reduction in overrepresentation of the small nation states elsewhere in Europe.

The three major parties differed considerably in their views, not so much on the nuts and bolts of allocation but in the way in which they placed their emphasis. For the Labour Party, the General Secretary pointed out that the size and composition of the Assembly had not been considered and that they were not committed to Direct Elections although the Government certainly was. The Conservatives wanted a British delegation of about 80 which would allow a 'reasonable' distribution of seats within the UK. The Liberals were the most specific, perhaps because they had made such an issue of the technicalities of Direct Elections, and, along with many others, hoped for as proportional an allocation of seats as possible (except for giving 5 seats to Luxembourg) and within an overall total of 350-400 seats. Despite the number of proposals under this heading, it seems that this was seen as a very dry area of debate compared to the more dramatic party battles going on over other issues.

To some extent, the main areas of interest were not related to the technicalities of the elections Europe-wide at all. This was shown during the speeches of British European MPs during the debates of 1975. Several Labour MPs expressed either outright rejection of Direct Elections or compounded difficulties such as the voting rights of British Nationals abroad suggesting that if they were included in the election Canadian, South African, Pakistani, Maltese etc., British nationals would have to vote as well as British nationals living in the EEC, while the Conservatives on the whole tried to balance this with wide ranging expressions of outright support, while the SNP argued their specific interests. It would be wrong to suggest that the British European MPs were alone in this, however, although with the exception of Denmark the majority of Governments in Europe were presiding over a continuing pro-European public. The parties responded to this on the whole, whereas the British delegation followed events in Britain itself by subsuming nearly all the technical issues outside electoral systems under a wealth of more general debate.

Conclusion

Hopes and Fears

The dilemmas of producing a directly elected delegation for the European Parliament from Britain, while to a large extent a result of the number of technical problems produced by the arrangement of the United Kingdom into areas of different regional politics and the balance of national politics at the time, were also related to much vaguer considerations many of which were more a question of nervous anticipation of the event than concern over specific issues. It is interesting to ask again just how unique Britain was in this respect, and it is likely that neither of these types of arguments themselves provided a precedent whereas the net result of their combination in Britain probably did. The resignation of Leo Tindemans from his position in the Belgian Government, for example, due to terrible splits over a proposal to divide the country into lingual regions proves that Britain's regional minorities have been less dramatic in their influence than some British observers concerned over the power of Westminster may have realised. Equally, as has already been shown, anti-Market opinion at the level of the general public and in politics was both evident and influential in Denmark and France. The persistent reiteration of arguments dating back to the earlier days of the 'European' idea was not unique in Britain either as a quote from a joint Socialist and Communist declaration of ten years ago in France shows,

Parties reaffirms its hostility to the setting up of a supranational authority created and dominated by capital, as it would accentuate the division of Europe, aggravate the baneful consequences for the workers of the present policy of the Common Market, and leave the democratic policy the French people want to the mercy of reactionary foreign governments . . . a little supranational Europe would be left dangerously under the sway of an expansionist and revanchist Germany and delivered to American tutelage . . .'[20]

The fear of German expansionism provides some comparison for the attitudes of the anti-Market British lobby, fighting for reversion to the nation state on the Left and a looking back to Empire on the Right, in that neither of them are new arguments in any sense. However, what is new in the French Communists is their attempt in some quarters to view Europe as a

Conclusion

fait accompli which must be dealt with from the inside, a result, perhaps of what is now many years of experience of the EEC. For the Left in Britain, however, this comment from the National Executive of the Labour Party of 1950, shows that there has been little or no change of tune despite the fact that almost any current calculations of the likely balance of parties in the elected Assembly would prove the probability of a Socialist majority which is likely to be very long-lived.[21]

No Socialist Party with the prospect of forming a government could accept a system by which important fields of national policy were surrendered to supra-national authority, since such an authority would have a permanent anti-Socialist majority and would arouse the hostility of European workers.[22]

There remains amongst several leftist parties in Denmark and Communists in Luxembourg the feeling that the EEC has nothing to do with Socialism and is likely, if anything, to hinder its progress. And it is in Denmark with its recent entry into the EEC and its decline in public support for further progress in 'Europeanism' under a Socialist government which provides the closest parallel to Britain's situation. In Denmark it could be that they decide to hold their elections for the national Parliament on the same day as those for the European Parliament. Whereas similar plans in Luxembourg and Holland are likely to be pro-European moves in as much as it is the European elections which were organised first and whose date is being respected, in Denmark's case there could well be an element of reserve in their decision, allowing as it will a good opportunity for the reintroduction of Europe in national politics and almost a rerun of the Referendum. Finally, as has been shown, legislative attempts to prevent incremental increases in the EPs powers were not only not original in Britain but were probably better executed in France.

Britain's individuality, although not demonstrated in the concrete terms above, was certainly real. It resulted more from her curious combination of a gloriously independent past and current economic weakness and the way in which such a transformation was translated into national politics than from anything really contemporary. As such, there should be no surprise that many of the arguments raised were not only not new since the Referendum but not new since the post-war period. For this reason also, perhaps, the power of the European assumed such importance in the debate and showed up, to some extent Britain's obvious inexperience in European affairs as they are currently constituted.

The debate over powers was a fine illustration of the old adage that one man's meat is another man's poison. Almost without exception the advocates of Direct Elections supported them on the grounds that they would provide a new impetus to 'Europeanism', would make the Parliament more effective and legitimate and would eventually lead to increased powers. This can be illustrated by comments both from the recent debates in Britain and from the debates of the 1960s in Europe. In 1969, the European Federalist Movement were very keen to 'open the door to general elections for the European Parliament and to the constituent phase of the nucleus of a federal European'. Elections were an especially important ideal at the time when the merging of the Communities was being discussed. The Europa Union of Germany as early as 1960 suggested, 'Only if the Parliament is truly democratic will it be possible to take foreign policy and defence policy measures in a Community spirit and to rule out the technocratic trends that can develop in the economic sphere.'[23] So while the pro-European extremists crowed about institutional development and the anti-extremists became nervous about national sovereignty it was obvious that no solution could please everyone.

The power of the European Parliament was, therefore, the butt of both the hopes and fears expressed over Direct Elections, being sent round and round in debates in Europe of the 1960s like chicken/egg, powers/elections, tending to reduce some pro-Europeans to extreme frustration as shown by Mr. le Hodey in 1960,

Before holdings elections it is argued, let us increase the Parliament's powers. This is a facile suggestion sometimes made by people who do not want to see an increase in the powers either of the Parliament or of the European Institutions. This seems to me to be a classic example of a pointless precondition.[24]

Going back to the British role, in fact was a very important factor since to a large extent there was a division in Europe between those who had been able to get or to continue to hope for developments which justified their reasons for joining and those who were beginning to feel, or had long felt that this could never occur. In Germany the essentially strategic nature of a United Europe was to be of enormous advantage in addition to the legitimacy which the EEC conferred on her after the War. In France, however, the existence of a very nationalistic lobby was bound to influence both her effect in Europe, making the Common Agricultural Policy, for example well tailored to French interests, and her ability to support continuations of moves of a Constitutional nature. In Britain, support for the Common Market had, in the referendum debate been based on a number of hopes but especially that of economic prosperity, pointing out the benefits which the economies of the EEC members had achieved, and the necessity for scale in a world of super powers. While the Left was concerned about the political implications of joining in the days of Britain's original application, both the introduction of the 'terms of entry' debates and the subsequent difficulty of explaining the causes of a serious crisis by the mid-seventies meant that the opponents now had new weapons. While the most evident signs of disaffection have emerged since the discussions over the format for Direct Elections there is no doubt that disaffection existed before and had been active in producing a rare combination of constitutional, economic and historical confusion over what to do about Europe. It is likely that if there are going to be groups classed as extremists over Europe in future, the most likely candidates are the outright supporters of Federal Union.

This analysis suggests that one really has to look both beyond and behind Direct Elections to find some rationale for much of Britain's behaviour. The frequent use of technical difficulties for essentially political ends by the anti-Market lobbies has meant that while the issue has raised a number of important problems which required investigation it has also meant that on occasion matters have been made unnecessarily complex. This was well noted by Mr. Patijn one of the major architects of Direct Elections in Europe, who said in 1977 'Elections do not have to win beauty contests. They simply have to take place'.[25] For the opposition this could be rewritten as 'beauty is in the eye of the beholder and democracy in this form may have an appeal which is, at best, deceptive, if not actually dangerous'. Either way the elections will now take place 18 years after the first real move to make them a reality and 22 years after the ink dried on Article 138, under conditions which will ensure that neither lobby will be satisfied. For the opposition, the first round will mean the losing of one battle in a war, and to the proponents it will mean the failure to achieve any advance towards a common system with the possibility of its early introduction receding fast. There are no coherent plans for the increase of the Assembly's powers but there are a number of obstacles preventing either increases in powers or a further reduction in the idea of national delegations in favour of truly European elections. Both these views show that the debates are far from over. Indeed, they will probably continue into the discussions over the common system, a further reassessment of national weighting, and the adaptation of new EEC members, with the second bout of enlargement not far off. While new members, at least, will probably produce some fresh insights into the elections and their role will thus inevitably be balanced by a re-run of the rest of the debate from those, like Britain, who seem to be exporting their propensity for continual reflection.

Footnotes

1. The arguments put forward by LAGER are shown in the appendices to the Minutes of Evidence taken before the Select Committee on Direct Elections to the European Assembly, Vol. II, pp. 51-58, 3 August 1976, HMSO.
2. They refer here to Explanatory Statement to Article 2 of the Patijn Convention. For a full discussion of the Convention and its contents see 'The Case for Elections to the European Parliament by Direct Universal Suffrage', Directorate General for Parliamentary Documentation and Information, the European Parliament, September 1969.
3. The Report of the House of Lords Select Committee states in paragraph 48 'the existing British system . . . might produce results more obviously unproportional (for 81 constituencies) than in 635 constituencies'.
4. See Debates of the House of Commons, 29 March 1976, *Hansard*, Vol. 908, No. 79, col. 905.
5. See paragraph 507 in the Minutes of Evidence taken before the Select Committee of the House of Commons on Direct Elections to the European Parliament, May-July 1976, HMSO.

Footnotes

6.   See paragraph 509 of the Minutes of Evidence, ibid.

7.   For a review of the merits and demerits of PR see *Adversary Politics and Electoral Reform*, ed. S.E. Finer, Anthony Wigram, 1975, especially Chapter One.

8.   See paragraphs 524-530 of the Minutes of Evidence in note 5.

9.   See the evidence of the LAGER group as referred to in note 1.

10. See paragraphs 47-48 of the Third Report of the House of Commons Select Committee on Direct Elections to the European Assembly, Session 75-6, 14 October and 9 November 1976, HMSO.

11. See Debates of the House of Commons, 24 November 1977, *Hansard*, Vol. 939, No. 16, Col. 1861.

12. See *The Times Guide to the House of Commons, October 1974*, Times Books, London, 1974.

13. See Appendix No. 50, p. 102, in appendices to the Minutes of Evidence taken before the Select Committee (as in note 1).

14. See *Independence and Devolution: The Legal Implications for Scotland*, ed. J.P. Grant, W. Green and Son, Edinburgh, 1976, especially T.S. Bates' chapter 'Devolution and the European Communities'.

16. See Appendix 25 of the Minutes of Evidence taken before the Select Committee (as in note 1), pp. 62-64.

17. As for note 13.

18. See *Official Journal of the European Communities*, No. 214 for 12th March 1969. These are the debates in plenary session on the notion for a resolution to elect members of the European Parliament.

19. See *Official Journal of the European Communities*, No. 368 for January 1975.

20. See the Joint Declaration of the FGDS and the PCF of 26 February 1968, published in *A Survey of European Documentation*, January-March 1968.

21. See H. Rattinger and M. Zangle, 'Distribution of Seats in the European Parliament after Direct Elections: A Simulation Study', *European Journal of Political Research*, Vol. 5, No. 3, September 1977, p. 201; and *Eurobarometer*, July 1977, for two attempts to predict the political balance of the European Parliament after Direct Elections.

22. Extract from U. Kitzinger's *The Second Try: Labour and the EEC*, Pergamon Press, Oxford, 1968. Section A (p. 59), 'A Statement by the National Executive Committee of the British Labour Party', May 1950.

23. This is an extract from the 12th Congress of the Europa Union of Germany held in Kiel, 26-30 May, 1961, produced in the monthly *Bulletin of European Documentation*.

24. See Debates of the European Parliament, 10 May 1960, reprinted in 'The Case for Elections to the European Parliament by Direct Universal Suffrage', ibid., p. 130 ff.

25. See *Official Journal of the European Communities*, No. 218, for 15 June 1977, p. 137.

Chapter 7

The Parties and the Direct Elections

Supra-National Groupings

In the European Parliament members sit in six supra-national political groups, rather than in national delegations. These groups, together with the independents, were made up as follows in the nominated parliament of 1978: Christian Democrats — 53 members; Communists and Allies — 18; Conservatives — 18; Liberals and Democrats — 23; Progressive Democrats — 16; Socialists — 66; Independents — 4. (*Source:* European Elections Briefing, European Parliament.)

Following agreement by the Nine on the holding of direct elections to the European Parliament, several groups have established more formal multinational parties or federations in order to fight the elections on a Community wide basis.

Christian Democrat Group: The European Peoples' Party; the Federation of Christian Democratic Parties of the European Community

The group dates from 1953 and the European Peoples' Party was formed in 1976 from the liaison committee set up in 1971 by the group and the European Christian Democratic Union.

Although based on a nineteenth century intellectual tradition, Christian Democracy has come to mean different things in different places and in different languages. The parties from Italy and the Benelux countries are centrist and wary of the right-wing German parties which together with some other Christian Democrats are also members of the European Conservative Union. The French Centre des Démocrates forms part of the new Giscardian Union pour la Démocratie Française, which includes liberals and conservatives. The party's constitution states:

> ... that the objectives include further European integration and 'the transformation of Europe into a European union with a view to achieving a federal union'.

It also laid down that a congress should meet every two years to which each member party sends delegates in proportion to the number of seats in the European Parliament. Between congresses decisions are taken by a political bureau in which each party has at least two votes, plus extra votes in proportion to its seats in the European Parliament.

Chairman of the Party: Leo Tindemans (Belgium).

Members are: *Belgium* — Christian Social Party (PSC-CVP); *France* — Centre des Démocrates Sociaux (CDS); *Germany* — Christian Democratic Party (CDU), Christian Social Union (CSU); *Ireland* — United Ireland Party (Fine Gael); *Italy* — Christian Democratic Party (DS), South Tyrol Peoples' Party (STVP); *Luxembourg* — Christian Social Party; *Netherlands* — Christian Democratic Appeal.

Communists and Their Allies

Communist Party members in the European Parliament, from France, Italy and the Netherlands, together with their Danish allies, have worked together as a group since 1973, for administrative purposes only, and Communist leaders have said that no supra-national party is to be established. The official line is that Communist parties have their specific characteristics in each country; their collaboration cannot be an attempt to achieve absolute identity of views and it must not lead to the creation of a 'European Communist Party'.

Each Communist delegation stands for what it perceives to be national interests, but generally the Communists work for major changes in the EEC. They oppose political integration, greater power to the Commission or the European Parliament and any weakening of the national sovereignty of the member countries. Thus the French leader, Georges Marchais claims that real and solid European cooperation presupposes respect for national independence, and that the Communists aim 'to remove European cooperation from the sole logic of profit and to make it an instrument to serve our country and its people'.

Chairman: (from 1973) Georgio Amendola (Italy).

The Parties and the Direct Elections

European Conservative Group, and the European Democratic Union (EDU)

After Britain's entry into the EEC, the British Conservative Party tried to form a right of centre supra-national group but failed to link up with the Christian Democrats. The Conservative Group at the European Parliament has been limited formally to the British and Danish Conservative parties. However, several Christian Democratic parties, and even some so-called Liberal and Progressive parties, share the Conservatives' political ideology, and in April 1978 the European Democratic Union was formed by ten parties, five of them from EEC countries. A further eight parties, including two from EEC countries, adopted the status of observer or 'permanent observer' to the EDU. The Christian Democratic parties of the centre-left refused to join, and the EDU may thus threaten the future of the EPP. Furthermore, the new alignments of the French Gaullists, and the French Republicans (as observers) with the EDU pose questions as to the future of the Progressive and Democratic Group and the Liberal Group.

The EDU stand *inter alia* for democracy, a pluralist society, the rights of man and the rejection of totalitarianism. In a speech to the Salzburg meeting the British Conservative Party leader, Margaret Thatcher, said that the EDU was 'the first and vital step towards an effective working alliance' of centre and centre-right parties against 'the Marxist threat to freedom' and would provide 'a forum within which we can discuss the problems which affect us all, whether we are inside or outside the (European) Community'.

President of the EDU: Dr. Josef Taus (Austria).
Members of the European Conservative Group: *Denmark* — Conservative Peoples' Party; *United Kingdom* — Conservative Party.
Members of the EDU: *Denmark* — Conservative Peoples' Party; *France* — Rassemblement pour la République; *Germany* — Christian Democratic Party (CDU), Christian Social Union (CSU); *United Kingdom* — Conservative Party.
Further members outside the EEC in Austria, Finland, Norway, Portugal and Sweden. Observers include South Tyrol Peoples' Party (Italy) and Parti Républican (France).

Introduction

European Progressive and Democratic Group
Formed originally in 1965 as the European Democratic Union, the group adopted its present name in 1973 when the French Gaullists who were the founders and dominant members of the group were joined by the Irish Fianna Fail, together with one of the small Danish parties. The Gaullists established an individualistic policy, hostile to political integration, during the de Gaulle era, but the Fianna Fail might easily have fitted into the Christian Democratic group if their Irish rivals, Fine Gael, had not got in before them. In 1978 Fianna Fail, for reasons of domestic policy, was seen to question its alliance with the Gaullists, whose membership of the EDU and the consequent link with the British Conservatives was seen as a compromising political association.

In 1973 the group as a whole had reached agreement on policy regarding the common agricultural policy, regionalism and social policy, but beyond that the member parties remained free to express their own opinions.

Chairman: (from 1973) Yvon Bourges (France).
Membership: *Denmark* — Progress Party; *France* — Rassemblement pour la République; *Ireland* — Fianna Fail.

Liberal and Democratic Group: Federation of Liberal and Democratic Parties of the Community
The Federation was founded in 1976 by leaders of fourteen Liberal parties from eight of the nine EEC countries, and the Liberal Group dates originally from 1953. In 1975 the British Liberal Party determined not to join the proposed federation because of the possible inclusion of the centre-right French Giscardian Parti Républican. Nevertheless, the body now embraces both British Liberals and the French Republicans, although the latter manage also to be 'permanent observers' to the Conservative EDU.

Although a small party in the European Parliament, the British Liberals have become influential in the supra-national group.

The manifesto adopted in 1976 by the Federation called for

. . . legislative powers for the European election of the European Parliament according to the principles of proportional representation; and

123

accountability of the European Commission to the European Parliament and the Council of Ministers.

It also stated that European union needed a common foreign policy covering the external relations of the Community and political cooperation designed to serve — together with the partners in the Atlantic Alliance, notably the United States — the freedom and security of Europe.

The Stuttgart meeting also unanimously adopted an emergency resolution proposed by the Netherlands party which declared that 'it would be an outrage to European opinion were the British Government to employ the electoral system currently used for Westminster elections for the first European elections', adding that such a procedure 'would return a British delegation even less representative of public opinion than is now achieved'.

President of the Federation: Gaston Thorn (Luxembourg).
General Secretary of the Federation: Florus Wijsenbeck.
President of the Group: Jean-Francois Pintat (France).
General Secretary of the Group: Massimo Silvestro.
Members: *Belgium* — Partij voor Vrijheid en Vooruitgang (PVV), Parti des Réformes et de la Liberté de Wallonie (PPLW); *Denmark* — Venstre (V); *France* — Parti Républican (PR), Mouvement des Démocrates-Sociaux de France (MDSF), Partie Radical Socialiste (RS), Apparentes UDF (App. UDF), Mouvement des Radicaux de Gauche (MRG); *Germany* — Freie Demokratische Partei (FDP); *Italy* — Partito Liberale Italiano (PLI), Partito Republicano Italiano (PRI); *Luxembourg* — Parti Démocratique (PD); *Netherlands* — Volkspartij vor Vrijhed en Democratie (VVD); *United Kingdom* — Liberal Party (Lib).

Socialist Group: Confederation of Socialist Parties of the European Community
The group was first formed in 1953, and the present confederation dates from 1974. The British Labour Party was not a member until 1976, after the referendum on United Kingdom membership. The group's general rule of only one member party per country means that several small left of centre parties are excluded from membership, and there is considerable divergence of views among the Socialists over cooperation with other parties, particularly the Communists, and over the commitment

Introduction

to European political integration. The three parties from Britain, Ireland and Denmark which were all hostile to some degree to Common Market membership have challenged the policies of the group and its attitude towards the future development of the Community.

At a Socialist Summit of the Nine in June 1978, a common 'Political Declaration' was adopted, and this committed the group to the common goals of freedom, social justice, equality and harmonious economic development. Working parties have been set up to formulate policy on human rights, employment and the enlargement of the Community. The group stresses that cooperation should be compatible with respect for each other's individuality, that trade unions should participate in the policy-making process and that the EEC, including its regional and social policies, should be geared to the equitable distribution of income, knowledge and power.

Chairman of the Group: Ludwig Fellermaier (Germany).
Secretary General: Manfred Michel.
President of the Confederation: Robert Pontillon (France).
Members: *Belgium* — Belgian Socialist Party (PSB-BSP); *Denmark* — Social Democratic Party; *France* — Parti Socialiste (PS); *Germany* — Social Democratic Party (SPD); *Ireland* — Labour Party; *Italy* — Democratic Socialist Party (PSDI), Italian Socialist Party (PSI); *Luxembourg* — Socialist Workers' Party (POSL); *Netherlands* — Labour Party (Pvd A); *United Kingdom* — Labour Party (Lab), Social Democratic and Labour Party (SDLP).

The one member per country rule is relaxed for Italy, where the right wing and left wing Socialists form separate parties, and the United Kingdom, where the Socialists of Northern Ireland have separate status.

The Parties and the Direct Elections

Belgium

BELGIAN SOCIALIST PARTY, Parti Socialiste Belge (PSB), Belgische Socialistische Partij (BSP)
Address: Maison du BSP, 13 Boulevard de l'Empereur, 1000 Brussels
Date of establishment: 1885
Representation in Belgian parliament (1978): 58 deputies and 52 senators
Officers (1978): André Cools (French president), Willy Claes (Flemish president), André Leonard and Gerrit Kreveld (secretaries)
Publications: Le Peuple, Vooruit, Volksgazet.
Originally called the Parti Ouvrier Belge, the PSB-BSP developed its strength in industrial areas, mainly in the French-speaking (Walloon) areas, and among co-operative societies and trade unions of the Fédération Générale des Travailleurs Belges (FGTB). It has campaigned for the extension of the franchise and social reform, and against fascism. Its programme is one of democratic socialism and integration within Belgium and the EEC.

CHRISTIAN SOCIAL PARTY, Parti Social Chrétien (PSC), Christelijke Volkspartij (CVP)
Address: 41 rue des Deux Eglises, 1040 Brussels
Date of establishment: 1945
Representation in Belgian parliament (1978): 82 deputies and 70 senators
Officers (1978): Charles Ferdinand Nothomb (president), Franz Swaelen (secretary)
Publications: ZEG/Tele-ZEG, Lettre à chacun, Action, Provincie en Gemeente/Province et Commune
Originally the Roman Catholic Party, the PSC-CVP upholds Church interests but includes non-Catholics among its 200,000 members. Strongly backed by the Christian trade unions, the party favours considerable social and economic reform. It manages to represent the interests of both the working class and representatives of commerce and manufacturing industry.

COMMUNIST PARTY, Parti Communiste de Belgique (PCB), Kommunistische Partij van Belgie (KPB)

126

Belgium

Address: 29-31 avenue Stalingrad, 1000 Brussels
Date of establishment: 1921
Representation in Belgian parliament (1978): 2 deputies and 1 senator
Officers (1978): Louis van Geyt (president)
Publications: Le Drapeau Rouge, De Rode Vaan, Cahiers Marxistes, Vlaams Marxistisch Tijdscrift
A small party, not significant in Eurocommunism.

FREEDOM AND PROGRESS PARTY, Partij voor Vrijheid en Vooruitgang (PVV)
Address: 39 rue de Naples, 1050 Brussels
Date of establishment: 1961
Representation in Belgian parliament (1978); the PVV, PL and PRLW *en bloc* have 37 deputies and 26 senators
Officers (1978): Pierre P. Descamps (president)
Formerly the Liberal Party, the PVV is based in Flanders and is generally conservative, favouring free enterprise, strong central government and tight controls on public spending.

FRENCH SPEAKING FRONT, Front Démocratique des Francophones (FDF)
Address: 42 rue P.E. Janson, 1050 Brussels
Date of establishment: 1968
Representation in Belgian parliament (1978); 10 deputies, and with RW shares 15 senators
Officers: Antoinette Spaak (president)
A language rights party, based in Brussels, the FDF was formed by members of the Mouvement Populaire Wallon and the Rénovation Chrétien Wallonne. The FDF joined forces with the RW in the 1968 election and had a common president until 1974.

LIBERAL PARTY, Parti Liberal (PL)
Based in French-speaking Brussels, the PL has been superseded by the PVV and the PRLW.

PEOPLE'S UNION, Volksunie
Address: 12 Barrikadenplein, 1000 Brussels
Date of establishment: 1954
Representation in Belgian parliament (1978); 14 deputies and

17 senators
Officers: H. Schiltz (president), P. Peeters (secretary)
Publication: Wij
The Volksunie is the Flemish nationalist party, which favours a federal state and seeks contact with other regionalist or nationalist parties in the EEC. It claims 560,000 members.

WALLOON FEDERALIST PARTY, Rassemblement Wallon (RW)
Address: 2 Place de Parc, 4000 Liège
Date of establishment: 1968
Representation in Belgian parliament (1978): 5 deputies and 15 senators shared with FDF
Officer: Paul-Henry Gendebrien (president)
The RW brings together the former Front Wallon, Parti Wallon and other French speaking federalist groups. The RW wants a federal state and it combined with the FDF in the 1968 elections. The RW is a left wing party, standing between the socialists and communists.

WALLOON LIBERAL PARTY, Parti des Réformes et de la Liberté en Wallonie (PRLW)
Address:
Date of establishment: 1976
Representation in Belgian parliament (1978): The PRLW, the PVV and the PL have 37 deputies and 26 senators between them
Officers: Willy de Clercq (chair), André Damseaux (president)
The PRLW embraces former members of the PVV, the PL and the RW. It seeks a federal state in Belgium and a united Europe.

Minor parties
German Speaking Belgian Party
Partei der Deutschsprachigen Belgier
United Feminist Party
Parti Feministe Unifie

Denmark

CENTRE DEMOCRATIC PARTY, Centrum Demokraterne (CD)

Denmark

Address: Folketinget, Christiansborg, 1218 Copenhagen
Date of establishment: 1973
Representation in Danish parliament (1978): 11 seats
Officer (1978): Erhard Jacobsen (chairman)
Publications: CD-Information, Centrum Avisen
A right wing splinter from the social democrats, the CD opposes ideological extremes and supports NATO and the EEC. Its members sit with the conservatives in the European parliament.

CHRISTIAN PEOPLE'S PARTY, Kristeligt Folkeparti (KF)
Address: Folketinget, Christiansborg, 1218 Copenhagen
Date of establishment: 1970
Representation in Danish parliament: 6 seats
Officer (1978): Jens Moller (chairman)
Publication: Idé Politik
Not part of the European Christian Democratic tradition, the party is interdenominational and stands against pornography and abortion.

CONSERVATIVE PEOPLE'S PARTY, Konservative Folkeparti (KF)
Address: 40 Vesterbrogade, 1602 Copenhagen
Date of establishment: 1916
Representation in Danish parliament: 15 seats
Officers: Jens Karoli (secretary), Poul Schuter (chairman)
Publication: Vor Tid
This is a small, urban based party which represents financial, industrial and business interests. It stands for protection of private property, adequate defence, sound fiscal policy and low taxation, but recognises the State's role in keeping the economic and social balance.

DANISH COMMUNIST PARTY, Danmarks Kommunistiske Parti (DKP)
Address: 3 Dr. Tvaergade, Copenhagen
Date of establishment: 1919
Representation in Danish parliament (1978): 7 seats
Publication: Land og Folk
The party first achieved representation in parliament in 1932 and took part in the coalition government after World War II. After 1956 the party was weak, pro-Soviet and without

representation in parliament. It is now uncommitted in the debate between Moscow and Eurocommunism.

EUROPEAN CENTRE DEMOCRATIC PARTY, Europaeiske Centrum Demokrater (ECD)
Address: Christiansborg, 1218 Copenhagen
Date of establishment: 1974
Representation in Danish parliament (1978): nil
Officer (1978): Lars Abel (chairman)
The party strongly supports co-operation with the EEC and promotes the dissemination of information about the Common Market.

INDEPENDENT PARTY, De Uafhaengige
Address: 5 Peder Skamsgade, 1054 Copenhagen
Date of establishment: 1953
Representation in Danish parliament (1978): nil
Officer: Swen Nielsen (chairman)

JUSTICE PARTY, Danmarks Retsforbund (DR)
Address: 1 Kroghsgade, 2100 Copenhagen
Date of establishment: c. 1920
Representation in Danish parliament: 6 seats
Officer: Ib Christensen (chairman)
Publication: Ret og Frihed
Traditionally known as the Single Tax Party, the DR follows Henry George's free trade teachings.

LEFT WING SOCIALIST PARTY, Venstre socialisterne
Address: 28B Skt. Pedersstraede (3rd), 1453 Copenhagen
Date of establishment: 1967
Representation in Danish parliament (1978): 5 seats
The party is a left wing offshoot from the Socialist People's Party (SF).

LIBERAL PARTY, Venstre
Address: 14 Hammerichsgade, Copenhagen V
Date of establishment: 1870
Representation in Danish parliament: 21 seats
Officers: Poul Hartling (chairman), Kurt Sorensen (secretary)
Publications: Fyns Tidende, Vestkysten, Frederiksborg Amts

Denmark

Avis
Originally called the Agrarian Party, the Venstre represents most farmers but also town dwellers and some businessmen. It is a right wing party and stands for individual self help against socialism and collectivism, government cut backs and a lowering of taxes, free trade and a minimum of government interference. It is the strongest supporter of the EEC among Denmark's parties.

PROGRESS PARTY, Fremskridtspartiet
Address: Folketinget, Christianborg, 1218 Copenhagen
Date of establishment: 1972
Representation in Danish parliament: 26 seats
Officer: Palle Tillisch (chairman)
Publication: Fremskridt
This right wing party was formed by Mogen Glistrup to protest against taxation and bureaucracy. It seeks the gradual abolition of income tax, the disbandment of most of the civil service, the abolition of the diplomatic service and the scrapping of 90% of all legislation.

RADICAL LIBERAL or SOCIAL LIBERAL PARTY, Det Radikale Venstre (DRV)
Address: DRV sekretariat, Christiansborg, 1218 Copenhagen
Date of establishment: 1905
Representation in Danish parliament: 6 seats
Officers: Svend Hangaard (chairman), S. Bjorn Hansen (general secretary)
Publications: Politiken, Skive Folkeblad, Holbaek Amts Venstreblad, Roskilde Tidende, Fremsyn
Traditionally the party of small landowners, urban intellectuals and professional people, the DRV stands for a strengthening of private enterprise in a welfare state. It has shared in numerous coalition governments, mainly with the Social Democrats. In the European parliament, the party was a member of the ELD but left because of its rejection of political integration.

SOCIAL DEMOCRATIC PARTY, Socialdemokratiet
Address: 26 Nyropsgade, 1602 Copenhagen
Date of establishment: 1871
Representation in Danish parliament (1978): 65 seats

Officers (1978): Anker Jorgansen (chairman), E.H. Christiansen (general secretary)
Publications: Vor Politik, Ny Politik
The largest political party, the Social Democrats represent trade unionists, industrial workers, white collar employees and public servants. The party stands for economic planning, full employment, extensive social security benefits and closer Nordic co-operation. Its leadership favoured entry into the EEC, but the 125,000 strong membership was deeply divided on the issue. Since joining the EEC, the Social Democrats have played a full part in its operations.

SOCIALIST PEOPLE'S PARTY, Socialistisk Folkeparti
Address: Folketinget, Christiansborg, 1218 Copenhagen
Date of establishment: 1959
Representation in Danish parliament (1978): 7 seats
Officer (1978): Gert Petersen (chairman)
Publication: Minavisen
A left wing body founded by former communists who opposed Soviet actions in Hungary in 1956, the party wants a socialist state, independent from the USSR, and calls for total, unilateral disarmament. It supports Nordic co-operation but opposes NATO and membership of the EEC.

Also: regional groups in Schleswig, Greenland and the Faroe Islands.

France

CENTRE DES DEMOCRATES SOCIAUX (CDS)
Address: 207 Boulevard Saint Germain, Paris 7e
Date of establishment: 1976
Officers: Jean Lecanuet (president), A. Diligent (general secretary)
This brings together the former Centre Démocrate and Centre Démocratie et Progrès. The CDS and the Parti Radical et Radical Socialiste acted together in the Mouvement Réformateur. The CDS supports the government of Giscard d'Estaing, represents the centre in French politics and strongly favours

European integration.

MOUVEMENT DEMOCRATE SOCIALISTE DE FRANCE (MDSF)
Address: 42 Boulevard Arago, Paris 13e
Date of establishment: 1973
Officer: Max Lejeune (president)
An anti-communist offshoot from the Parti Socialiste, the MDSF forms part of the Fédération des Réformateurs. The MDSF member of the European parliament has sat with the Liberals.

MOUVEMENT DES RADICAUX DE GAUCHE (MRG)
Address: 11 rue de Grenelle, Paris 7e
Date of establishment: 1973
Officer: Robert Fabre (president)
A left wing offshoot from the Parti Radical, the MRG co-operated with the Communists and Socialists of the French opposition.

PARTI COMMUNISTE FRANÇAIS (PCF)
Address: 2 place du Colonel Fabien, Paris 19e
Date of establishment: 1920
Representation in French parliament (1978): 74 deputies
Officer: George Marchais (general secretary)
Publications: L'Humanité, France Nouvelle, Cahiers du Communisme
The PCF claims 500,000 members and strong trade union support. It subscribed to a common programme of the United Left with the Parti Socialiste and favours the democratic road to socialism and an independent foreign policy. Although originally hostile to the EEC, the PCF has moved steadily towards Eurocommunism and a full role in the workings of the EEC, including acceptance of direct elections.

PARTI DES FORCES NOUVELLES (PFN)
Date of establishment: 1974
Officer: Pascal Gauchon (general secretary)
An umbrella for right wing parties and groups.

The Parties and the Direct Elections

PARTI RADICAL ET RADICAL SOCIALISTE (PRRS)
Address: 1 place de Valois, 75001 Paris
Date of establishment: 1901
Officers: Jean-Jacques Servan-Schreiber (president)
Publication: BIRS
This was a major party under the Third and Fourth Republics, anti-clerical but moderate in economic and social politics. With the Centre des Démocrates Sociaux, the PRRS formed the Mouvement Réformateur and supports the Giscard d'Estaing government.

PARTI REPUBLICAIN (PR)
Address: 41 rue de la Bienfaisance, 75008 Paris
Date of establishment: 1977
Representation in French parliament (1978): 62 deputies
Officer: Jean-Pierre Soisson (general secretary)
The PR represents the pro-Gaullists who split from the CNIP in 1962. The party succeeds the Fédération Nationale des Républicains Indépendants (FNRI), the party of President Giscard d'Estaing, and three other pro-Giscard parties. It represents groups of political clubs such as the 'Génération sociale et libérale' and 'Agir pour l'avenir'. It is pro-NATO and 'European' in its outlook.

PARTI SOCIALISTE (PS)
Address: 7 bis Place Palais Bourbon, Paris 7e
Date of establishment: 1905; reorganised 1969
Representation in French parliament (1978): 93 deputies.
Officer: François Mitterand (first secretary)
Publications: L'Unité, La Nouvelle Révue
The main non-communist party of the left, the PS grew rapidly after reorganisation in 1969, but joined with the communists in the United Left programme until 1977. Its policies include full employment, a planned economy and critical co-operation with the EEC.

PARTI SOCIALISTE UNIFIE (PSU)
Address: 9 rue de Borromée, Paris 15e
Date of establishment: 1960
Officers: secretariat of five
Publication: Critique Socialiste

A revolutionary left wing splinter group, the PSU was not part of the United Left.

RASSEMBLEMENT POUR LA REPUBLIQUE (RPR)
Address: 33 avenue du Maine, Tour Maine Montparnasse, 75755 Paris Cedex 15
Date of establishment: 1976
Representation in French parliament (1978): 171 deputies
Officers: Jacques Chirac (Hon. general secretary), Yves Guéna (general secretary)
Publications: La Lettre de la Nation, Démocrates, Les Cahiers
The main right wing pro-government group, the RPR is the Gaullist party and succeeds the 'Union des Démocrates pour la République'. The Gaullists once sat with the Liberals in the European parliament, but left in 1962 when de Gaulle began to attack supra-nationalism.

Minor parties and other groups
Centre Républicain (Fédération des Réformateurs)
Front National (right wing)
Ligue Communiste Révolutionaire (Trotskyist)
Lutte Ouvrier (Trotskyist)
Mouvement des Démocrates
Mouvement de la Gauche Réformatriçe (centrist)
Mouvement des Sociaux Libéraux (left wing offshoot from the RPR)
Mouvement Progrès et Liberté (Fédération des Réformateurs)
Nouvelle Action Français
Oeuvre Française (right wing)
Organisation Communiste Internationaliste
Parti Communiste Révolutionaire (Marxist-Leninist)
Parti des Forces Nouvelles (right wing)
Restauration Nationale (right wing)
Union des Communistes de France (Marxist-Leninist)
Also: regional parties in Brittany, Corsica, Provence, Languedoc and the Basque country.

The Parties and the Direct Elections

Germany

CHRISTIAN DEMOCRATIC PARTY, Christlich Democratische
Union (CDU)
Address: Konrad Adenauer Haus, Friedrich-Ebert Allee 73-75,
53 Bonn
Date of establishment: 1945
Representation in German Bundestag (1978): 254 seats with CSU
Officers: Helmut Kohl (chairman), Heinrich Geissler (general
secretary)
Publications: Deutsches Monatsblatt, Union of Deutschland
A generally conservative party of some 660,000 members, the
CDU seeks joint action of Catholics and Protestants in the re-
construction of German life on a Christian basis, guarantees for
private property, free enterprise and individual liberties, and a
'free and equal Germany in a free, politically united and socially
just Europe'. Its right wing stance has made it suspect to some
other Christian social parties.

CHRISTIAN SOCIAL UNION, Christlich-Soziale Union (CSU)
Address: 33 Lazarettstrasse 8, Munich 19
Date of establishment: 1945
Representation in German Bundestag (1978): 254 seats with
CDU
Officer: Franz Josef Strauss (chairman)
Publication: Bayernkurier
The equivalent to the CDU, operating in Bavaria, the CSU is a
more conservative party.

FREE DEMOCRATIC PARTY, Freie Demokratische Partei
(FDP)
Address: Thomas Dehler Haus, 15 Baunscheidtstrasse, Bonn
Date of establishment: 1945
Representation in German Bundestag: 40 seats
Officer: Hans-Dietrich Genscher (chairman)
Publication: Liberal
The FDP, which forms part of the SPD-FDP coalition govern-
ment, represents the political centre, policies of social liberalism
and individual rights. It exerts strong influence in the ELD in
the European parliament.

136

Ireland

GERMAN COMMUNIST PARTY, Deutsche Kommunistische
Partei (DKP)
Address: Dusseldorf
Represention in German parliament (1978): None
Officer: Herbert Mies (chairman)
The successor to the original West German Communist Party
which was banned in 1956, the DKP claims 40,000 members.

NATIONAL DEMOCRATIC PARTY OF GERMANY, National-
demokratische Partei Deutschlands (NPD)
Address: P.O. Box 2881, 7 Stuttgart
Date of establishment: 1964
Representation in German parliament: None
Officer: Martin Mussgnug (chairman)
Publication: Deutsche Stimme
A right wing party accused of neo-Nazi tendencies, the NPD
claims 40,000 members.

SOCIAL DEMOCRATIC PARTY OF GERMANY, Sozialdemo-
kratische Partei Deutschlands (SPD)
Address: 1 Ollenhauerstrasse, 53 Bonn
Date of establishment: 1945
Representation in German parliament (1978): 224 seats
Officer: Willy Brandt (chairman)
Publication: Vorwarts
Strongly based in the cities and industrial areas, the SPD stands
for strong central government, social justice, the improvement
of relations with Eastern Europe, maximum competition and as
much planning as necessary to protect the individual from an
uncontrolled economy. The party has lost its original Marxist
outlook and forms a coalition government with the Free Democrats. In the European Parliament, the SPD members have
dominated the Socialist Group, providing its leaders and funds.
The party remains cautious about European integration.

Ireland

LABOUR PARTY
Address: 16 Gardiner Place, Dublin 1
Date of establishment: 1912, reorganised 1930

Representation in Dail Eireann (1978): 17 members
Officers: R. J. Connolly (chairman), S. Scally (general secretary)
The party aims for an extension of public ownership, industrial democracy and improvements in the welfare state services. It opposed Ireland's accession to the Treaty of Rome but accepted the result of the referendum on EEC membership.

REPUBLICAN PARTY, Fianna Fail
Address: 13 Upper Mount Street, Dublin
Date of establishment: 1926
Representation in Dail Eireann (1978): 84 members
Officers: Jack Lynch (president), S. Brennan (general secretary)
Fianna Fail has held governmental responsibility for most of the time since 1932 and advocates a peaceful ending of Ireland's partition, social justice, national self sufficiency and a return to the Irish language. A conservative party, Fianna Fail sat with the Gaullists in the European parliament.

UNITED IRELAND PARTY, Fine Gael
Address: 16 Hume Street, Dublin 2
Date of establishment: 1933
Representation in Dail Eireann (1978): 43 members
Officers: Garret Fitzgerald (leader), Liam Cosgrave (president)
The Fine Gael, which formed a coalition government with Labour from 1973 to 1977, advocates friendship and ultimate unity with Northern Ireland, financial encouragement of industry, protection of foreign investment and agricultural development. In Europe, the party joined the EPP and the European Christian Democratic Union although it had no historic contact with Christian democracy.

WORKER'S PARTY, Sinn Fein
Address: 30 Gardiner Place, Dublin
Date of establishment: 1905
Representation in Irish parliament (1978): None
Officer: Tomas MacGiolla (president)
Publication: United Irishman
Sinn Fein has a Marxist programme for the ending of partition in Ireland and the creation of a Democratic Socialist Republic of All Ireland.

Minor parties
Communist Party of Ireland
Irish Republican Socialist Party
Republican Unity Party

Italy

CHRISTIAN DEMOCRATIC PARTY, Partito Democrazia
Cristiana (DC)
Address: EUR Piazzale Luigi Sturzo 15, 00144 Rome
Date of establishment: 1943
Representation in Italian parliament (1978): 265 deputies and
136 senators
Officer: Benigno Zaccagnini (general secretary)
Publications: Popolo, La Discussione
The DC, the party of government, is strongly anti-communist
but represents voters of all classes and attempts to take a
centrist position. It forms a 'wide church' of ultraconservatives,
moderates and social reformers. In the European parliament,
its role and influence has not been commensurate with its size.

COMMUNIST PARTY, Partito Comunista Italiano (PCI)
Address: 4 Via delle Botteghe Oscure, 00186 Rome
Date of establishment: 1921
Representation in Italian parliament (1978): 228 deputies and
116 senators
Officers: Luigi Longo (president), Enrico Berlinguer (general
secretary)
Publications: L'Unita, Rinascita, Critica Marxista, Politica e
Economica, Foreign Bulletin
The broad-based PCI is Italy's second largest party, claiming
1,715,922 members. It follows the parliamentary road to
socialism, seeking widespread economic, social and political
reforms to be implemented by a broad coalition of democratic forces. The party emphasises economic planning, social
services, development of the South and an independent foreign
policy. The pioneer of Eurocommunism, the PCI works within
EEC structures and favours European integration.

DEMOCRATIC SOCIALIST PARTY, Partito Socialista Demo-

cratico (PSDI)
Address: 12 Via Santa Maria in Via, 00187 Rome
Date of establishment: 1969
Representation in Italian parliament: 15 deputies and 6 senators
Officer: Guiseppe Saragat (president)
Publication: Umanita
A right wing offshoot from the Socialist Party, it first attained a separate identity in 1947 when it represented those socialists who refused to collaborate with the communists. It was temporarily reunited with the PSI from 1966 to 1969.

ITALIAN SOCIAL MOVEMENT — NATIONAL RIGHT, Movimento Sociale Italiano-Destra Nazionale (MSI-DN)
Address: 22 Via Quattro Fontane, 00184 Rome
Date of establishment: 1946
Representation in Italian parliament (1978): 33 deputies and 15 senators
Officer: Alfredo Covelli (president)
Publication: Il Secolo d'Italia
A neo-fascist party in the tradition of Mussolini, the MSI-DN sat with the Liberals of the European parliament until 1972. It claims 400,000 members.

ITALIAN SOCIALIST PARTY, Partito Socialista Italiano (PSI)
Address: 476 via del Corso, 00186 Rome
Date of establishment: 1966
Representation in Italian parliament (1978): 57 deputies and 29 senators
Officers: Pietro Nenni (president), Bettino Craxi (general secretary)
Publications: Avanti, Mondo Operaio
The PSI dates from the nineteenth century and included the Partito Socialista Democratico Italiano from 1966 to 1969. It is the main non-communist party of the left and represents workers, and progressives of the middle class. The PSI stands for greater prosperity, freedom and social justice and believes that socialism is inseparable from democracy and individual freedom, but it has grown weaker vis-à-vis the communists. The PSI favours European integration.

LIBERAL PARTY OF ITALY, Partito Liberale Italiano (PLI)

Italy

Address: 89 via Frattina, 00187 Rome
Date of establishment: 1848
Representation in Italian parliament (1978): 5 deputies and 2 senators
Officers: Giovanni Malagodi (chairman)
Publication: La Nuova Tribuna
Founded by Cavour, the PLI stands for free enterprise and laicism. It takes a centre position in Italian politics, and supports NATO and the EEC.

PROLETARIAN DEMOCRATS (Avanguardia Operaia, Lotta Continua and the Partito di Unita Proletaria per il Comunismo)
Date of establishment: 1970s
Representation in Italian parliament (1978): 6 deputies
This was an umbrella for left wing parties in national elections and has increased its strength as the communists have become more pro-government.

RADICAL PARTY, Partito Radicale (PR)
Address: 18 Via Torre Argentina, 00186 Rome
Representation in Italian parliament (1978): 4 deputies
Officer: Adelaide Aglietta (secretary)
A moderate left wing party, the PR campaigns on civil rights issues.

REPUBLICAN PARTY OF ITALY, Partito Repubblicano Italiano (PRI)
Address: 70 Plaza dei Caprettari, Rome
Date of establishment: 1897
Representation in Italian parliament (1978): 14 deputies and 6 senators
Officers: Ugo la Malfa (president), Oddo Biasini (political secretary)
Publications: La Voce Repubblicana, La Voce de Romagna, Trapani Nuova, Partito e Societa, Oggi, Come, Il Lucifero, Il Corriere Nuovo, Noi Repubblicani, 30 Giorni, Libera Cooperazione
The PRI upholds Mazzini's principles of social justice in a modern free society. Small but influential, it stands left of centre and once sat with the Socialists in the European parliament.

The Parties and the Direct Elections

SOUTH TYROL PEOPLE'S PARTY, Sudtiroler Volkspartei (SVP)
Address: Passagio Vintler/Durchgang 16, 39100 Bolzano
Representation in Italian parliament (1978): 3 deputies and 2 senators
The SVP is the regional party of the strongly Catholic German-speaking minority.

Minor parties include
Committee for Public Defence (right wing)
Europe Civilization (right wing)
Manifesto Group (left wing)
Marxist-Leninist Party of Italy (left wing)
Movement for National Reconstruction (right wing)
National Front (right wing)
Potere Operaio (left wing)
Union of Italian Marxist-Leninist Communists (left wing)
Union Valdotaine (right wing)

Luxembourg

CHRISTIAN SOCIAL PARTY, Parti Chrétien Social (PCS)
Address: 38 rue de Curé, Luxembourg
Date of establishment: 1914
Representation in Luxembourg parliament: 18 seats
Officer: Jacques Santer (president)
Once called the Parti du Droit, the PCS represents farmers and Catholic workers. A conservative party with 7,500 members, the PCS is Luxembourg's largest grouping. It stands for political stability, planned economic expansion and support for the monarchy and for the EEC.

COMMUNIST PARTY, Parti Communiste (PC)
Address: 16 rue Christophe Plantin, Luxembourg
Date of establishment: 1921
Representation in Luxembourg parliament: 5 seats
Officer: René Urbany
A hard line pro-Soviet party.

DEMOCRATIC PARTY, Parti Démocratique (PD)

Address: 46 Grand'rue, Luxembourg
Representation in Luxembourg parliament: 14 seats
Officer: Gaston Thorn
The PD is Luxembourg's liberal party and a member of the government coalition. It was formed by moderates and conservatives who favoured a mixture of free enterprise and progressive social legislation. It is pro-NATO and supports the EEC.

SOCIAL DEMOCRATIC PARTY, Parti Social Démocratique Luxembourgeois (PSDL)
Address: P.O. Box 162, Luxembourg 2
Date of establishment: 1971
Representation in Luxembourg parliament: 5 seats
Officer: Henry Cravatte
Publication: FF (Freiheit und Fortschritt)
The PSDL is a right wing offshoot from the Socialist Workers' Party.

SOCIALIST WORKERS' PARTY, Parti Ouvrier Socialiste Luxembourgeois (POSL)
Address: 63 rue de Bonnevoie, Luxembourg
Date of establishment: 1902
Representation in Luxembourg parliament: 17 seats
Officers: Lydie Schmidt (president) and Robert Goebbels (general secretary)
A moderate Marxist party, supported by workers and trade unionists in urban areas, the POSL supports a welfare state, NATO and European integration. It shares in a coalition government with the PD.

Netherlands

CHRISTIAN DEMOCRATIC APPEAL (CDA)
Date of establishment: 1977
Representation in Dutch parliament (1978): 24 seats and 49 seats in the second chamber
Parliamentary leader: Ruud Lubbers
An umbrella in Holland and in the European parliament for the three Catholic and Protestant parties of the centre and right.

The Parties and the Direct Elections

CHRISTIAN HISTORICAL UNION, Christelijk Historische Unie (CHU)
Address: 7 Wassenaarseweg, The Hague
Date of establishment: 1908
Officers: Baron van Berschner (chairman), J. L. Janssen van Raay (general secretary)
Publications: Christelijk Historisch Weekblad, De Nederlander
A Protestant party, more progressive than the ARP and more working class.

CATHOLIC PEOPLE'S PARTY, Katholieke Volkspartij (KVP)
Address: 25 Mauritskade, The Hague
Date of establishment: 1945
Officer: W. Vergeer (president)
Publication: Politiek Nieuws
The major Roman Catholic party, claiming 55,000 members, the KVP favours social welfare co-operation between the spiritual and secular authorities. It is open to non-Catholics.

PROTESTANT ANTI-REVOLUTIONARY PARTY, Anti-Revolutionaire Partij, Evangelische Volkspartij (ARP)
Address: 3 Dr Kuyperstraat, The Hague
Date of establishment: 1879
Officer: H. A. de Boer (president)
Publications: Nederlandse Gedachten, AR Post, Anti Revolutionaire, Staatkunde
A conservative Calvinist party representing businessmen, white collar workers and farmers and claiming 60,000 members. It seeks religious influence on the community and opposes nationalisation and a planned economy.

COMMUNIST PARTY, Communistische Partij van Nederland (CPN)
Address: 324 Keizergracht, Amsterdam
Date of establishment: 1920s
Representation in Dutch parliament (1978): 2 seats and 2 seats in the second chamber
Officer: Henk Hoekstra (chairman)
Publications: De Waarheid, Politiek en Cultuur
A small party, generally uncommitted between Eurocommunism and allegiance to the Soviet Union.

Netherlands

DEMOCRATIC SOCIALIST PARTY, Democratische Socialisten
'70 (DS'70)
Address: 94 Herengracht, Amsterdam
Date of establishment: 1970
Representation in Dutch parliament (1978): 1 seat in the second
chamber only
Officer: Dr. Willem Drees
A right wing offshoot from the Labour Party.

DEMOCRATS 1966 (D'66)
Address: Amsterdam
Date of establishment: 1966
Representation in Dutch parliament (1978): 8 seats in the second
chamber
Officer: Mrs. R. E. van der Scheervan Essen
A left of centre reforming party, the D'66 members used to sit
with the socialists in the European parliament but are now
closer to the liberals.

LABOUR PARTY, Partij van de Arbeid (P.v.d.A)
Address: 31 Tesselschadestraat, Amsterdam-w
Date of establishment: 1946
Representation in Dutch parliament: 25 seats and 53 seats
Officers: Ien van den Heuvel (chairman), G. Heyne de Bak
(secretary)
Publications: Partij Krant, S. en D., Roos in de Vuist
A democratic socialist party formed by groups of progressive
Protestants, Catholics and Liberals and by the former Socialist
Democratic Workers' Party, the P.v.d.A has strongly supported
the EEC and European integration. It is now more left wing
than it used to be.

PEOPLE'S PARTY FOR FREEDOM AND DEMOCRACY,
Volkspartij voor Vrijheid en Democratie (VVD)
Address: 57 Koninginnegracht, The Hague
Date of establishment: 1948
Representation in Dutch parliament (1978): 15 seats and 28
seats in the second chamber
Officers: F. Korthals Altes (chairman), W. J. A. van den Berg
(general secretary)
Publication: Vrijheid en Democratie

145

The Parties and the Direct Elections

Undenominational and continuing the tradition of the former Liberal State and Liberal Democratic Parties, the VVD supports free enterprise together with social security and workers' shares in profits and management. It has been influential in the ELD.

RADICAL POLITICAL PARTY, Politieke Partij Radikalen (PPR)
Address: 277 Singel, Amsterdam
Date of establishment: 1908
Representation in Dutch parliament (1978): 5 seats and 3 seats in the second chamber
Publication: PPRAK (PPR-aktiekrant)
An offshoot from the Christian parties, the PPR is left of centre and collaborates with socialists and progressives. It tried to form a supranational radical group in the European parliament.

STATE REFORMED PARTY, Staatkundig Gereformeerde Partij (SGP)
Address: 21 Hooigracht, The Hague
Date of establishment: 1918
Representation in Dutch parliament (1978): 1 seat and 3 seats in the second chamber
Officer: Rev. H. G. Abma (chairman)
Publication: De Banier
A small part of fundamentalist Calvinists.

Minor parties include
Dutch Trades People's Party, Nederlandse Middenstands Partij
Farmers' Party, Boren Partij (1 seat in each chamber)
National Reformed Political Association, Gereformeerd Politiek Verbond (1 seat in each chamber)
Netherlands Roman Catholic Party, Rooms Katholieke Partij Nederland
Pacifist Socialist Party, Pacifistisch Socialistische Partij (1 seat in each chamber)

146

Chapter 8

Britain and Europe:
Current Issues and Controversies

Introduction

As previous chapters have outlined, Direct Elections themselves have been a very important and controversial issue in Britain. With the decision to participate in the elections must come a wider assessment of recent developments in Europe and how they have been received here. Party political cleavages over European policies have been poorly developed in Britain due to the continuing dominance of pro- and anti-Market biases in approaches to European affairs. It is possible to see where left and right wing reactions to individual policies will differ markedly with the implementation of some of the longer term ideas in the Community, the most obvious case being that of the future role of the Regional and Social policies. However, the extent to which true party political divisions will emerge in Britain over European policies will depend upon whether the momentum of anti-Market opinion within the Labour Party and the British electorate continues to grow and whether obvious divergences between the interests of Britain and those of the Community arise with greater or lesser frequency.

While the extent of anti-Market pressure within Britain has meant that no policies of the EEC have escaped analysis in terms of national costs and benefits, the consensus that the CAP must be reformed[1] is evidence of reduced gulfs between pro- and anti-Market viewpoints where a policy obviously transgresses British interests. Party political divisions, where they are evident, tend to reflect respective compromise positions arrived at through balancing pro- and anti-Market opinion within the party concerned. The example of the Labour Party shows that such compromises are far from simple and cannot be

147

equally applied to all aspects of EEC policy.[2] Specific policies tend to be used by anti-Marketeers as illustrations of the iniquity of the Common Market, whereas, for some pro-Marketeers, recent developments such as fisheries policy and the EMS have tended to raise doubts over some of the implications of further European integration. This chapter will review several major areas of EEC policy juxtaposing the views of the EEC itself and British attitudes.[3]

Agriculture

Agricultural policy has loomed so large in British press and media reports of EEC affairs that it can truly rank as one of the most controversial aspects of Britain's membership. The debate centres on the CAP itself as a means of controlling production, prices and markets in agricultural produce, especially where these are seen as being related to, and in contravention of, British interests. As with fisheries, the negotiations over the CAP have been not only a vehicle for those already strongly anti-EEC but they have also made many who were neutral or pro-EEC at the time of the Referendum increasingly dubious about it. It is one of the most advanced areas of European supranational organisation and has had great impact upon domestic policy-making with seemingly endless proposals and directives for controlling the food market coming before the British public. This, in itself, has caused serious damage to the credibility of the policy as a whole.

Although since the Referendum, there has been a consensus among pro- and anti-Europeans alike over the need to reform the CAP,[4] the term 'British interests' is still understood very differently by both sides. Most anti-EEC critiques of the CAP dwell upon the deficiency payments as the proper way to organise farm supports and consumer prices. British interests are equated with a return to the past and an espousal of home-grown policies. For pro-Europeans, British interests are seen as being properly served by allowing a rapid development towards European integration, believing that those aspects of membership which will favour Britain should be allowed to balance the effects of the CAP as soon as possible. Much of the difficulty in this argument has been the fact that EEC policies remain very unbalanced with expenditure upon agriculture dominating the EEC budget at the expense of other policies, particularly in the regional and social fields. The fact that benefits of membership have been slow to manifest themselves has meant that for pro- and anti-Europeans alike the CAP poses a real contravention of British interests, although for different reasons.

The Labour Party has been split over agricultural policy. Despite a hard speech from James Callaghan on the CAP and the EEC budget in November 1978, it is clear that the methods of John Silkin have not appealed to many pro-Europeans in the party. However, numerous conference resolutions, a history of strong action and plenty of adverse media coverage of the CAP will provide firm backing for a ferocious attitude towards the future of the CAP. John Silkin's dramatic negotiations have often been reported in heroic terms and several newspapers, e.g. the *Guardian*, have taken a firm stand against the CAP. The paper says:

> The *Guardian* has always argued that the CAP is perverse and foolish, that it works in favour of the big producer and against the interests of the consumer, that it is wrong because it is protectionist and that in a hungry world it generates absurd surpluses of food at prices which no one can afford to pay.

Wine lakes and butter mountains are now well-established in the vocabulary of the EEC, particularly since there have been several well-publicised instances of such surpluses having been sold off at reduced prices to the Eastern bloc.[6] To the leadership, reform has now become a precondition for cooperation in other spheres such as the EMS,[7] but for the anti-EEC lobby within the party abolition of the CAP has become urgent and a precondition for remaining in the EEC at all.[8]

For the largely pro-European Conservative Party, agriculture may well receive criticism, as an easy, unpopular issue with which to present a more balanced view of Europe to an increasingly disenchanted British electorate. As the eurobarometer on Direct Elections[9] has shown, the majority of the British electorate is going to want their European MP 'to support the interests of (their) country all the time whether or not they are good for Europe as a whole'. With the pro and anti lobbies being forced closer together in their criticism of the CAP it is likely that, in this sphere at least, the majority of the British electorate will have cause for celebration after the election.

Although the image of the CAP has made the whole of the

EEC seem intransigent and frequently to deny British interests, the real cause for the bitterness lies in less recent events. The most important point is the fact that the CAP was designed around French interests, inasmuch as it was meant to be a means of modernising small, inefficient farms, without creating massive rural unemployment, while ensuring a rise in agricultural incomes commensurate with those of industry. As the only exporter of food on a large scale within Europe at the time, France had the prospect of a large and growing market for its goods and the growth in production would therefore be absorbed within a walled garden of high tariff barriers. From a British point of view, it is difficult to understand the strength of the agricultural lobby being so great as to influence major areas of policy. However, at the outset of the European experiment, France had over a quarter of her population engaged in agriculture. Agricultural reform, jointly financed at the European level, was therefore an important factor in easing the pain of lost national sovereignty. As Michel Debré explained in a speech in 1960,[10] 'Does the desire to have a common agricultural policy among the member states of the EEC amount to a weakening of Europe? The common agricultural policy is provided for in the Treaty and this helped to gain support for the Treaty in the French Parliament.' For a nation like Britain, with a highly efficient agricultural sector and the highest level of food imports in the Community, the formulation of an agricultural policy would be very different.

From the early post war days,[11] discussions in Britain of European union dwelt at enormous length on the need to protect the interests of the Commonwealth. Not surprisingly, many of de Gaulle's arguments that Britain was not yet ready for entry were formed on the basis of Britain's dependence upon agricultural and other trade links with her ex-colonies.[12] With people looking back to the days when Commonwealth trade actually meant importing relatively cheap food in large quantities (especially dairy produce and sugar), the argument has now become one of rising prices due to the inability to import as cheaply as before and accusations of a closed mentality which allows the EEC to damage the interests of third world and other outsiders, such as Yugoslavia.[13] The importance of food prices in Britain in recent years has been evidenced by the enormous reluctance of John Silkin to devalue the green pound, since this mechanism can be used to increase the cost of EEC agricultural imports but prevent increases in farm prices at home. It is important to realise that food prices play a much less important role in the politics of the original Six. Since the proportion of income spent on food has fallen in these countries,[14] it is not surprising that they feel consumer interests are being protected in other spheres and that agriculture (in the form of the CAP) is little more than a mild irritation.

The EEC is acutely aware of the extent to which ill-feeling is being generated by the CAP amongst British policy-makers and electors. In presenting its case, rare instances occur of the need to justify what is usually heralded as a bastion of European co-operation.

The accession of the United Kingdom added a further dimension — and new problems — to the efforts to strike a fair balance between the demands of farmers and consumers. Since the CAP came into operation, food prices have fluctuated less than they have elsewhere. Some critics of the policy say that this has been achieved at a cost of keeping prices artificially higher than world prices but some premium has to be paid for such a reliable insurance policy . . . Higher productivity has in some cases led to surpluses, but these are difficult to avoid, while guaranteeing that enough food is produced.[15]

Fisheries

Together with agriculture, fisheries have been a prime focus for recent wrangles over the national interest. Attempts to create a Common Fisheries Policy have been seen as a move to give EEC fishermen carte blanche in the well-stocked waters around Britain, except for a small inshore zone which would remain for British fishermen only.[16] A prime consideration has been the need for conservation measures in view of the very serious depletion which has taken place in some species such as herring. One result of the failure to reach agreement at the EEC level has been a unilateral ban on herring fishing brought into force by John Silkin without acquiring the consent of the other Eight. British interests obviously diverge from those of other EEC members given the concentration of many of the most popular types of fish in waters which have traditionally been fished by the British. The only major control on fishing which has been achieved outside the herring ban has been the introduction of licensing and quota control of non-EEC fishermen within a 200 mile zone. This was aimed particularly at the 'factory ships' of the Japanese and the eastern bloc, particularly Russia, which were seen as a major threat to the conservation of stocks in the future.

The controversy over how large an area of exclusively British waters could be allowed within a Common Fisheries Policy has been another major battle waged by John Silkin. As with agriculture, he has been seen here as an important protector of British interests, although this is not a view held by other members of the EEC. After one recent breakdown in talks, West German government officials were reported as having suggested[17]

It seems quite clear that by ensuring the failure of these talks Mr. Silkin wants the whole question to go to the Common Market Summit here on December 4th and 5th (1978). It seems that his strategy is to resign if Mr. Callaghan comes back from the summit with an agreement he does not like and then head up the anti-Market forces in the Labour Party.

Whatever the verity of such conclusions, it is clear that Britain has frequently followed up suggestions that agreement was very close with a peremptory slamming of the door. As early as 1976, EEC Bulletins[18] were expressing the hope that an agreement was not far off. In July 1978, in the European Parliament, Lord Kennet[19] explained that they were within 'half an inch' of success in the negotiations. He went on to explain some of the background to Britain's difficulties in respect of fisheries,

... when Britain joined the Community ... a policy was drawn up amongst the existing six members which it was not possible for Britain to accept. There was consequently a classic, long-run battle between Britain and the others, during which positions were taken up ... which are now proving extremely difficult to abandon ... it is perhaps habit rather than any intrinsic difference which allows the conflict to continue.

The EEC has now accepted the overwhelming need for conservation. However, within overall controls on fishing, the aim of a common policy will be to have equal access for all Community members with certain weightings of quotas being provided for those who have historically been associated with particular areas. Certainly, the attitude of John Silkin, while greatly concerned with the overall level of stock depletion, has in fact been equally concerned to prevent European Unity advancing to a point where the Nine could achieve common maritime boundaries. Although losing the 1975 Cod War with the Icelanders made a strong British attitude over fisheries inevitable, it is likely that a Conservative administration would have conceded issues of sovereignty more quickly and quietly, but still retained a concern for the level of stock depletion. As with other EEC policies, anti-Marketeers, like John Silkin, would have a vested interest in showing that the EEC could not work in Britain's interest. The majority of the pro-Marketeers would see the protection of these interests as being secondary to allowing European unity to progress. With an issue like fisheries, these differences of principle can be more closely seen in the manner of negotiation if not always in the arguments expressed. These highly technical arguments can easily be reduced to discussion of the scientific validity of particular sets of data.[20]

The EEC in presenting its own case over fisheries, has placed great stress on the role of fisheries policy in creating a common approach to foreign policy as well. For instance, the Soviet Union was forced to negotiate with the EEC to grant licences and quotas to non-EEC members to be able to fish in Community waters. The EEC's common front was seen again when it acted as a single negotiator on the Law of the Sea Conference.

Progress has been difficult with both fisheries and agriculture. Rather than blaming a political attitude for the disagreement, the EEC suggest that 'vastly divergent traditional interests of the individual Member States', together with differing dependence on inshore rather than deep sea fishing, as well as different eating habits, are the causes. Much more likely is the fact that each country, in differing degrees, finds it difficult to accept the way in which its EEC membership affects national interests. What is a good policy for two or three countries may be bad for another. Disagreement is not confined to British negotiators only. One can expect further dissension since the EEC is currently trying to reach agreement with Spain over fisheries prior to membership[21] and finding that it is just as problematic as the British negotiations. However, the strength of feeling generated by fisheries negotiations in the British camp will be hard to match. The fact that the breakdown in talks on 24 November 1978 went against the specific instructions of both James Callaghan and Helmut Schmidt[22] to their respective ministers, may cause a state of anarchy from which it will be very difficult to develop any agreement or order.

European Monetary System

This policy has produced a very wide divergence of reaction in Britain in both pro- and anti-European circles. Discussion has been tempered with strong feeling on both sides of the debate and there has been considerable controversy, e.g. Brian Sedgemore (once Parliamentary Private Secretary in the Department of Energy) was dismissed for the acquisition and 'leaking' of a confidential Cabinet document drawn up by the Treasury explaining numerous disadvantages of Britain's involvement with EMS. To some extent, because the mechanisms whereby EEC currencies would be held in closer parity with one another are so complex, the political and media debate has restricted itself to the more emotional and wider political considerations, rather than a real tackling of the economic issues involved.

A plea for a longer term analysis of the implications of the EMS for Britain was made in an article by Robert Skidelsky[23] where three major questions were outlined; self-sufficiency versus interdependence, globalism versus regionalism, and the role of fixed exchange rates as an internal discipline. Tracing the changing position of Britain from the 16th century, Skidelsky concludes that the degree to which interdependence is required depends to a great extent upon which territorial unit one considers to be 'the nation'. If one considers, as List did, that the nation is simply any territorial unit in which formal agreement exists to prevent war and commercial restrictions, it is obvious that nationhood rests with the EEC. The fundamental disagreements between pro- and anti-Marketeers could well be phrased in these terms; the former taking a much more restricted view of nationhood and the latter moving towards views such as List's. If interdependence is seen as inevitable then it is necessary to ask whether such links should be regional (i.e. European) or global. Skidelsky considers that the extent to which it is possible to have global interdependence depends upon the existence of superpowers. Certainly, global versus regional interdependence was Britain's major choice when joining the EEC, given that the Commonwealth was an important, albeit declining, determinant of British trade at the time. In the case of the EMS, the reality of Britain's position is that there are few alternatives to a European level of cooperation. Despite the strength of anti-Market feeling here and elsewhere, the vague alternatives of uniting Eastern and Western Europe in a demilitarised zone[24] or of isolation and protectionism at home are rarely assessed in the public forum as viable solutions.

It is the EMS as an internal discipline which has been the main focus of debate, together with the underlying assumptions about loss of national sovereignty and the lack of political will within the Labour Party to consider any further moves towards European Unity.

Recent history is illuminating in that it shows the developing role of exchange rates as internal discipline. Prior to the period between 1964 and 1967, decisions on whether exchange rates should be fixed or floating were not in the least contentious, the desirability of fixed rates being taken for granted. After the frantic attempts to avoid devaluation in 1964 and again in 1967, the situation changed from one where one fixed rate had been substituted with another to one where a floating currency became increasingly attractive. This is particularly true of the period from 1972-76 if only because it had become impossible to hold any fixed rate of sterling. However, the appropriateness of stability of exchange rates was never questioned, the implication being that stability of the exchange rate depended upon stability within the economy as a whole. Under these new circumstances fixed exchange rates clearly involve some restrictions upon the domestic policies of the United Kingdom government. During the periods 1964-67 and 1970-72 it became clear that unrealistic exchange rates were incompatible with 'Keynesian' economic policies aimed at full employment through high public expenditure. Inability to devalue under these conditions would result in a leap in unemployment through a reduction in public expenditure, whereas inability to revalue (if the rate were artificially low) would possibly increase the rate of inflation.

Given that these two outcomes straddle the two most important evils of the British economy today, fixed exchange rates obviously present a real challenge to British policy-makers. However, it should be added that devaluation has certainly not been a sufficient measure against these problems, especially where there is a high level of imports. Large sections of the Labour Party have, therefore, both political and economic grounds for opposing the EMS, given their commitments to prevent further moves towards European integration, to ensure full employment and to increase public spending. For monetarists, such as Sir Keith Joseph of the Conservative Party, neither the economic nor the political implications of EMS would pose such a serious problem.

The *Financial Times*, however, rightly pointed out[25] that the EMS need not actually mean a fixed exchange rate. Italy, for example, had negotiated a 6% margin around its central exchange rate resulting in an overall band of 12% between the strongest and weakest currencies. Even the Government's own Green Paper[26] on EMS pointed out that in the last 22 months (from November 1978) the sterling effective exchange rate had remained within 61.5% and 63% of its 1971 level, a band of less than 3%. Under these circumstances, the effect of EMS membership upon overall domestic policy would not be very marked. The real question is whether the future of sterling is likely to be more or less stable than its recent performance. For this reason, many have argued that a decision not to join the EMS would be a vote of 'no confidence' in the future of sterling and the British economy as a whole.

The fact that further moves towards European integration necessitate moves towards greater stability between European currencies has made most anti-Marketeers against EMS stand alone, but the pattern within the Cabinet over EMS is not one of a straight pro- versus anti-Market division. This is because there will be, for example, different long term and short term effects of the EMS. The type of short term effects envisaged depend to a great extent upon whether the new regime would mean a higher or lower exchange rate for Britain. A higher rate would certainly mean that competition for foreign markets would be tougher due to an increase in the price of exports. A lower rate tends to have an overall inflationary impact by increasing the prices of imports. This can offset whatever advantage has been gained in the export field by restricting wage rises. As the Green Paper points out,

In recent years, however, the effect of changes in nominal exchange rates seems to have been slower and less certain. In some countries the volume of exports has held up in a striking way in spite of sharper exchange rate appreciation and lower costs offset much of the effects of appreciation. The Government for its part has made it clear that it does not regard exchange rate depreciation as a solution to the economic problems still facing the United Kingdom.[27]

The EEC, in presenting its case, suggest that the EMS 'is a very important step' and that 'progress towards economic and monetary union can make a decisive contribution to the achievement of the common national objectives of stability, growth and employment'. In short, they suggest, 'It is a recipe for action in bad times as well as good.'[28] They rightly point out, however, that the EMS cannot be isolated from the short term economic policies within the Nine and that through other policies there will be a redistribution of funds between the richer and poorer nations. The anti-Marketeers and those most dubious of the EMS feel that moving towards economic policies similar to those pursued in Germany is a very good reason for leaving the EMS alone. Those enthusiastic about the EMS and European Union see this as a golden opportunity for renewed momentum and, as with EEC membership as a whole, a sure way of preventing the fulfilment of some of the more extreme socialist measures which the Labour Party NEC might wish to include in future manifestos.

The *Guardian*, reporting on the 1978 Labour Conference, produced an idiosyncratic analysis of the discussions at that time:

What is depressing about the debate so far is the way in which the freedom to devalue seems to have been made, at least in the view of the Treasury, into the last outpost of the Empire . . . There is force in the argument of those who say that given the grossly inferior performance of the British economy by comparison with the West German, there is no way in which a currency stability zone can either work or serve the British interest. The Labour Party's NEC managed to make this deplorable fact, if fact it is, sound like some kind of national triumph. Perhaps it thinks we should be kept in quarantine for fear of catching the German disease.[29]

One's conclusions on the suitability of EMS for the British economy will to a great extent depend upon whether one feels that the 'German disease' will work to Britain's advantage or detriment, how one feels the inflation rate will change, closing or widening the gap with Germany, and whether depreciation is a necessary tool of Government in combating (or avoiding) some of the more unpalatable problems in the British economy. Prestige enters the debate because second class membership of the system may be a compromise which would alienate both

CurrentIssuesandControversies

Current Issues and Controversies

European enthusiasts who feel that Britain will exert more influence over Europe's direction as a full member, and anti-Marketeers who feel that any involvement would fly in the face of official Labour Party policy. Given the highly technical nature of the economics involved, the politics of prestige and protectionism are likely to predominate the continuing debate over how the EMS is handled.

Regional Policy

Since the beginning of European integration it was felt that the effect of free competition within the Community would aggravate rather than ameliorate regional imbalances within it. The fact that the Regional Fund was only set up in 1975 shows the extent to which other policies have been accorded higher priorities, the adverse effect which economic depression has had upon regional problems and regional unemployment in particular, and the effect of the first enlargement of the Community. The ECSC Treaty, recognising the importance of the coal and steel sector with regard to regional decline, did provide funds for industrial conversion and re-training. The amounts are: £556m being spent on re-training and £178m loaned for re-conversion so far. Prior to the creation of the Regional Fund, other policies designed to redress regional imbalances have come as part of the Agricultural Guidance policies for farm modernisation, Social Fund allocations for re-training those faced with redundancies, and the work of the European Investment Bank, where 75% of its funds are being directed towards investment in poorer areas.

The Regional Policy itself is administered by national administrations. The grants made for specific projects submitted by national governments are still fairly small as compared with the extent of regional aid given by national governments themselves. In 1975-77, the first three-year period of the Fund, £520m was allocated although a further £1,447m has been allocated for 1978-80. An explanation for the small amount of aid being allocated is given by the EEC itself when it explains, 'A key requirement is that money from the Fund should be additional to national expenditure and not be used simply to reimburse national authorities'.[30] A careful balance is being created, therefore, between regional redistribution at the EEC level and that at the national level. When compared with agriculture where support at the national level has been almost

158

totally taken over by action at European level and where ten times the amount of funds go, Regional Policy is still at a very early stage of development.

With the exception of Greenland, it is the periphery of Europe which is in greatest need of regional aid. There are very different views as to how such imbalances could be redressed. In Corsica, Brittany, Northern Ireland, Scotland and Wales the reaction has been to press for autonomy from their national governments, but in the latter case this has been coupled with a certain optimism over the possible role which the EEC can play in providing diplomatic, political and above all financial support. The Left view regional policy as part of a wider scheme of redistribution with regional imbalance being associated with capitalist development, as are inequality of income, power and information. Following a meeting of the leaders of the Socialist parties of the European Community in June of 1978 the following Declaration was proposed:

We Socialists will continue to strive for a more equitable distribution of income and wealth. We note with particular concern that efforts to assist the development of the Community's less favoured regions have made little headway. We therefore demand a clear and vigorous regional policy designed to reduce differences in living standards between the various regions in the Community. At the same time we demand an effective social policy capable of removing the many inequalities between groups of citizens in our countries.[31]

The implications of a really effective regional policy were outlined in a 1977 Report of the Commission of the EEC in the 'Role of Public Finance in European Integration'.[32] The report produced figures of the ratio of GDP (Gross Domestic Product) per capital between the richest and poorest countries of the EEC (2.2 in 1975) and between the richest and poorest regions within countries (being between 1.6 and 1.8 within countries such as Germany, France and Britain). However, 40% of these disparities were eliminated within individual nations through the mechanisms of public finance. Most of the reduction in disparities was achieved by progressive personal taxation, social security transfers and biases in public expenditure programmes. Very little was achieved through policies specifically labelled 'regional'. The conclusion drawn was that there could be an equal levelling of regional disparities at the European level if the Community Budget was increased from the 1977 rate of

0.7% of Community GDP to 2.5%. Most of this would be achieved by a transfer of public spending from national to Community level, rather than by actual spending increases. This type of suggestion would probably not find much support amongst British anti-Marketeers (of the Left) given that it would involve a considerable transfer of power to Community level and would not involve an overall increase in the level of redistribution. Equally, as the regional problems of both Italy and Ireland are more serious in many ways than those of Britain, it could mean an actual reduction in the type of regional support provided to British regions by British taxpayers. From the EEC and pro-European viewpoints, however, such a policy would have much to commend it given that it would provide greater momentum at Community level and an answer to critics of the current Regional Fund, without involving an overall increase in expenditure.

As far as the future of the Regional policy is concerned, therefore, there will be pressure from the Left for strengthening mechanisms whereby inequalities may be reduced. In Britain this is not likely to be popular unless there is little or no increase involved in the power of the Community. For the Right and other pro-Europeans there is a general consensus that European Union cannot be furthered in an atmosphere of excessive regional disparities in the same way that progress may be halted by exchange rate disparities. The extent to which the Right would sanction large increases in public spending and further progressive taxation to achieve this end is unlikely to be very great. The general aim of regional policy is not controversial but neither side is likely to allow uncomfortable sacrifices to be made in order to achieve it.

Social Policy

The activities of the Social Policy, like those of the Regional Policy, have not been a source of great contention in Britain and have been designed as a counterbalance to the worst excesses of free competition. The areas of concern in 1977, although concentrated around employment policy, also covered sex equality, living and working conditions, vocational training, and social welfare and health. There have also been moves in industrial relations and discussion of industrial democracy. Much of the work of the Social Policy, loans and grants etc., has been research, with twenty-five studies being undertaken examining the labour market alone, and Heads of Departments meetings. These also involved Ministers of Health and Employment.

Specific aid to Britain has gone to the coal and steel industries helping to fund early retirement to the tune of 1,722,750 units of account (u.a.). Low cost housing schemes under the ECSC received 33.56m (u.a.). Under the Social Fund, 110 schemes were devoted to the United Kingdom in 1977. These were divided between agriculture, textiles, migrant workers, young people, the handicapped and developing regions with funds going to private firms and government agencies alike. Half of the projects were devoted to regional development, especially the Northern Ireland Manpower Services Commission, Regional Training Services Agencies and some to the Highlands and Islands Development Board.

The mechanism of distribution of Social Fund aid is similar to that of the Regional Fund; both are related to specific projects and are administered by national governments. Many of the same political considerations also hold. Being a much less developed area of Community policy compared with agriculture, the real locus of social policies rests with national governments and the sums spent are correspondingly small. The development of a more powerful social policy is envisaged by the EEC itself which has said:

In both the regional and social fields, it is no longer sufficient for Community funds to be limited to a complementary role . . . This . . . implies a greater transfer of resources for which political support at the Community level must be found. A directly-elected European Parliament will provide a vehicle for mobilising this essential support for more active Community financial intervention.[33]

Whether the elected Parliament will perform this task single-handed is arguable, given that there will be a continuing division between those who wish to make Europe work as a unit and those who will work to ensure that there is no increase in Community intervention in national policies.

The support of strong interventionist measures is a political issue with which British electors are well acquainted, but the addition of the national sovereignty issue complicates the matter considerably. It is possible therefore that those who would argue most strongly for a strong Social Policy at home would oppose it as strongly at Community level. Equally, there will be many in the Conservative Party who would find it difficult to support expansion in the social sphere at home under present circumstances, but would welcome such expansion at Community level. To some extent, therefore, sectoral policies are still seen as pro- or anti-European rather than Left or Right wing. Some signs that this pattern was changing did emerge from the Socialist leaders' declaration,[34] when they said '. . . the Community must now advance to a new phase in which the emphasis — in policy and in action — will be changed from the dictates of commercial interest to the pursuit of humane and cooperative goals'. The Declaration was agreed to by the Labour Party but this does not mean that questioning Britain's membership is no longer complicated by views on Social Policy.

External Relations

There have been a number of external issues in the Community in recent years. Indeed, growing discussion of foreign affairs, e.g. the European Parliament's debating of Orlov's trial, the Camp David agreement, the Lebanon and Human Rights in Argentina in 1978 are all part of a growing desire to present the EEC as an outward looking organisation capable of presenting a united front on foreign affairs. Although the chaotic involvement of Belgium and France in Zaïre's war in the copperbelt did nothing to complement these moves, declarations have been produced recently showing a common view of the Palestinian question and of South Africa. A common foreign policy will probably be a long-term process. However, more recent foreign affairs have been concerned with economic dealings with the Third World, energy policy, and preparations for a further enlargement of the Community.

Aid to the Third World is organised around the Lomé Convention of 1975, now called the Lomé Policy. This was originally seen as a resolution of the problem of post-colonial trade relations between EEC members and countries in the developing world. However, agreements have now been reached which broaden this picture considerably. Foremost amongst these have been the agreements with Mediterranean countries including Tunisia, Egypt, Israel and Jordan, and the so-called Group of '77 which includes every developing country in the world and to which are accorded certain trade preferences. The generalised preference system involves selective reductions in tariffs of imported agricultural goods and the duty-free entry of manufactures and semi-manufactures under certain quota restrictions. The total of tariff exemptions for 1978 has been estimated at £217m but it should be noted that many of the products involved do not compete directly with those of the EEC producers and that the total amount involved is very small given the huge area over which it is distributed. There are schemes for food aid also. These are sent to the areas of greatest need and during emergencies such as earthquakes and cyclones. Although the EEC is criticised for not helping as much as it could towards the development of a new economic order on the one hand and in offsetting the effects of its trading policies in New Zealand, for example, the EEC itself is well aware of the need to do more. Although certain countries such as Botswana have a large and growing trade deficit with the EEC, the developing world as a whole has a trading surplus with the EEC which amounted to about £12,000m in 1976 out of an overall trading volume of over £74,000m.

Energy policy also has been an important factor in foreign policy and the EEC hopes, for example, that it will be able to bargain with OPEC with a single voice. Britain, however, would find it difficult to go along with a common European argument for lower oil prices, since her position as an oil producer and a future oil exporter means that her interests lie with higher rather than lower prices. Internally, Britain will resist attempts to create preferential treatment for EEC importers of British oil and it will therefore be difficult for the EEC to create a common energy policy internally as well as externally. Although the anti-European views of Energy Minister, Tony Benn, have not made Britain's attitudes any more accommodating, there is nonetheless an obvious divergence of interests which will not change whether the negotiators concerned are pro- or anti-Market.

Enlargement of the Community has raised several questions amongst existing and applicant members alike. The entry of Greece, Spain and Portugal into the EEC would certainly produce a number of difficulties especially in the fields of agriculture and regional policy. The large agricultural populations and low agricultural productivity in all three applicant states will mean that financial aid to modernise them will result in overproduction and the creation of surpluses. Certain products, especially wine, citrus fruits and some vegetables will create a threat to existing producers of these commodities in France and Italy. However, for 'northern type' agricultural products the entry of three new members will be welcomed because there will be a growth in demand without a reduction in their price to the consumer. At present the CAP favours northern over southern European agriculture and there will certainly be pressure for this to be changed when three new southern members arrive. Already the French and Italian producers of wine, fruit and vegetables are getting financial aid to give them a competitive edge over their Portuguese, Spanish and Greek counterparts. The French and Italians are likely to ensure that the Treaties of Accession for these applicants will include clauses preventing growth in production of goods which compete with their own.[36]

Under these circumstances, it will be difficult for the farmers of the applicant states to increase their incomes through increases in production or through competing successfully with producers in existing member states. Any increased profitability will have to depend upon greater efficiency and this in turn will mean a large reduction in their agricultural populations, but this cannot happen until other sectors of their respective economies grow fast enough to absorb this new workforce. Despite difficulties, all three countries, especially Greece, have been trying to adapt their economies to the EEC system in advance of membership. In Portugal this has meant serious reconsideration of the role of private capital in a highly nationalised economy, at a time when they are already having to conform to economic pressures from the IMF. In all three countries, they have had to prove themselves capable of adapting to the aftermath of dictatorship and the introduction of universal suffrage.

Politically, Greece's application has presented problems for the future of the EEC's relationship with Turkey. Formally, the EEC has explained that it is Greece's problem, not theirs;[37] but there are signs that Greece is having to improve relations through the exchange of prisoners and renewed negotiations over the Aegean. To some extent Greece's relationship with NATO is also involved, since both Britain and Germany see the EEC as an important underpinning of NATO. The possibility of Greece becoming a full member again will very much depend upon whether they can save face with Turkey in other ways and the extent to which left-wing anti-NATO pressure in Greece gains the ascendency.

Institutionally, it seems that the EEC is ill-adapted to the prospect of further enlargement when still trying to deal with the reverberations of the original enlargement. Many feel that it will be difficult to operate in a Council of 12 Ministers without the introduction of majority voting. But this could damage the interests of the smaller states whose lack of power and population have been balanced by equal voting power in the Council up till now. Since Britain and France are opposed to further encroachments on their national sovereignty, they would be bound to oppose a move to remove the power of the veto.

Regionally, the enlargement will involve a considerable upheaval in the balance of rich and poor areas within the Community. The demand for increased redistribution of funds will certainly grow since any enlargement will increase regional disparities at a time when the Community's present operation is not succeeding in balancing free competition and regional aid. Britain will be looking for allies in the new members to support her in her arguments for reform of the CAP and in trying to balance the demands of regional aid with the need to encourage free enterprise. Whether the EEC should change its emphasis from wealth creation to redistribution and whether this would benefit the Community is a question which will have great bearing on the operation of the European institutions, especially the Parliament, by the mid-1980s. With EEC documents already referring back to the extent of common ground reached within the original Six[38] as compared with the present Nine, the operation of a Community of Twelve may well find that any common ground achieved will be the exception rather than the rule.

Competition Policy and Implementation of the EEC Treaties

Setting up a customs union within the EEC and the establishment of a common external tariff on imported goods was aimed at allowing the free movement of goods within the Community. However, obstacles to totally free competition such as State aid to selected industries, different standards of packaging and safety of goods and the means of marketing products such as milk, have necessitated continual proposals for 'harmonisation' and a watch dog role for the European Commission from the end of Britain's transitional period in 1977. Many of the Commission directives have been seen as excessively petty and trivial in Britain. The attempt to abolish the Milk Marketing Board in favour of action at Community level was especially disapproved of by farmers who felt that this would alter Britain's position as the leading consumer of fresh milk in the EEC.[40] In the end the Commission decided upon a referendum (a very unusual move) but felt that only if 80% of milk producers owning more than half the country's cows voted to retain the existing system would the result be accepted. As it was the majority was well over 80% and the system will remain the only means of marketing British milk. This, however, is a rare case where harmonisation will not be achieved through the imposition of directives.

Regional policies which are felt to excessively favour entire industries or entire member states are also frowned upon and aid to specific industries such as the pig producing industry was halted. Those who feel that the creation of totally free trade within the Community will adversely affect weaker areas of the British economy at a time when recession is already creating real difficulties can point to the currently low levels of aid being granted for the counterbalancing policies in the social and regional fields. The EEC itself feels that there are benefits from free competition in the sphere of controlling big business.

The aim of (the) competition laws is to prevent large firms abusing a dominant position in the market or to prevent firms from forming cartels by means of which they can rig prices or restrict distribution . . . Certain mergers can also be banned if they endanger competition . . . Public ownership as such is not contrary to Treaty rules. However, State monopolies of a commercial character are banned and since 1962 the Commission has succeeded in eliminating most of the 18 which existed at that time.[41]

One's assessment of the potentialities of free competition within the EEC must rest with one's view of the EEC as a whole. It is primarily an economic community and thus establishment of free trade is one of the main pillars upon which the Treaty is is based. Restrictions upon state aid, controls and ownership obviously make the EEC Treaty a political instrument in as much as it points to a future of larger scale stronger capitalist development, rather than the achievement of full-blooded socialism.[42] The extremists of the Left are appalled at this prospect but those of centrist persuasions find it appealing. The fact that harmonisation for Britain has occurred at a time of high unemployment, with support for weaker sectors of the economy becoming politically unavoidable and with a Labour government in power, has thus put competition policy in a damaging light. The alternative to the pursuit of the Treaty Implementation in this respect is not, as in the case of agriculture, reform, but ending British membership; since there can be few compromises in achieving a customs union and free movement of goods and capital.

One major consideration in implementing the Treaty obligations concerned Britain's contribution to the EEC budget. The Prime Minister made an issue of this in November 1978 when he criticised the Community for giving Britain an unfair deal. Although it is very difficult to produce objective statistics of the real net contribution of individual states, Mr. Callaghan certainly believed that Britain was, unjustly, the greatest net contributor to EEC revenue. It is estimated that from 1979 Britain's net contribution will be nearly £800m per annum. This seeming imbalance is due to the fact that 70% of Community funds go towards agriculture and thus benefit Ireland and Denmark at the expense of the rest. Britain feels indignant that the distribution of benefits within the Community should be so irrational as to aid almost the richest and poorest countries of the Community at the expense of Britain herself. Arguments have raged over the level of contributions of Member States for the 1978 Budget and Britain may well embellish her image of non-cooperation during future negotiations over contributions. This would almost certainly be the case whatever government were in power, especially since those favourable to the EEC are not helped by wide publicity of this unfortunate inequity.

Footnotes

1. See *The Spectator*, 14 November 1975, 'CAP: The Case for Reform'.
2. See Chapter Four.
3. 'The European Community Today and Tomorrow', produced by the Office for Official Publications of the European Communities in February 1978, was designed as a guide to the activities of the EEC for British electors with Direct Elections in mind. Quotes of EEC

views, therefore, come from this publication although most of the statistics come from more specialised publications related to specific policies.

4. *Spectator*, 15 November 1975, ibid.
5. *The Guardian*, 25 November 1978. For the vocabulary of the EEC, see Chapter 2.
6. *The Guardian*, 22 November 1978, 'Iron Curtain butter deal on'.
7. See the Government Green Paper, 'The European Monetary System' Cmnd 7405, November 1978, HMSO.
8. For examples of Labour views from different sections in the party, see *The Times*, 23 May 1976, *The Economist*, 8 October 1977, and *The Times*, 1 October 1977. See also 'The Common Market: The Cost of Membership', Labour Common Market Safeguards Committee, 1977.
9. *Eurobarometer*, No. 7, produced by the Commission of the EEC, 4 July 1976.
10. From a speech by Michel Debré at Metz, 2 October 1960.
11. See Chapter One.
12. See the speech made by President de Gaulle at a press conference at the National Press Club, Washington, 23 April 1960. This is reprinted in PEP, Occasional Paper No. 11, 30 January 1961, Metchim and Son, London.
13. *The Guardian*, 25 November 1978, 'The Wider Shadow of the CAP'.
14. See 'CAP Still Under Attack', the *Financial Times* supplement on Europe, 4 December 1978.
15. 'The European Communities Today and Tomorrow', ibid.
16. The proposals for a Common Fisheries Policy were aimed at achieving a 12 mile limit for exclusive use of the coastal nation, a further 12 mile limit allowing limited use to EEC members and an overall 12 mile limit with strict controls of third party fishermen.
17. *The Times*, 25 November 1978, 'EEC fishing talks collapse with harsh words on all sides'.
18. See the Tenth General Report of the Activities of the European Committee, February 1977, p. 163.
19. Lord Kennet's speech appears in the Debates of the European Parliament sitting of 6 July 1978, *Official Journal of the European Communities*, No. 232, p. 238.
20. Lord Kennet's speech, ibid., p. 236.
21. See Debates of the European Parliament sitting of 15 September 1978, *Official Journal of the European Communities*, No. 233, p. 271 ff.
22. See *The Times*, 'EEC fishing talks collapse with harsh words on all sides', ibid.
23. The article referred to is 'Euro-money: self-sufficiency or interdependence?' in *New Society*, 30 November 1978.
24. See extracts from *The Second Try* by U. Kitzinger, Pergamon Press, Oxford, 1968.
25. The *Financial Times*, 30 November 1978, 'EMS: missed chances and false trails'.

26. See Cmnd 7405, ibid.
27. See Cmnd 7405, ibid.
28. 'The European Community Today and Tomorrow', ibid.
29. *The Guardian*, 5 October 1978, 'Labour's sullen resistance to Europe's economic sense'.
30. 'The European Community Today and Tomorrow', ibid.
31. From the declaration following a meeting of the Heads of the Socialist Parties of the European Community on 23-24 June 1978. Confederation of the Socialist Parties of the European Community.
32. See the Report of the study group on 'The Role of Public Finance in European Integration'. The Commission of the European Communities, Brussels, 1977. For an examination of the difficulty with which the Parliament can increase regional and social spending, see *The Guardian*, 22 November 1978, 'Britain in clash with Germany on EEC Budget'.
33. 'The European Community Today and Tomorrow', ibid.
34. Confederation of the Socialist Parties of the European Community, ibid.
35. See Debates of the European Parliament, Official Journal of the European Communities, Nos. 232-234.
36. See the *Financial Times* supplement on Europe, 4 December 1978.
37. See 'Opinion on Greek Application for Membership', *Bulletin of the European Communities Supplement*, 2/76, the Commission of the European Communities, 1976.
38. 'The European Community Today and Tomorrow', ibid.
39. See *The Times*, 25 November 1978, 'Dairy raspberry blown at Brussels'.
40. 'The European Community Today and Tomorrow', ibid.
41. This view would be much more widely held in the British Labour Party than amongst many other Socialist Parties of the EEC. Their joint declaration (ibid.), for example, states that a reduction in inequality must necessitate a change in 'the economic and social structures in our countries. We realise that whilst each country can by itself do much towards this end, joint action between us in some fields can accelerate the process'.

Chapter 9

The Voting: Analysis and Prospects

Introduction

For the Direct Elections, the United Kingdom has been divided into 81 Euroconstituencies. Of these 66 are in England, 8 in Scotland, 4 in Wales and 3 in Ulster. Except for the special case of Ulster, all will elect MPs on the first-past-the-post system. The final boundaries for these constituencies were announced on 24 November 1978. On 4 December they were finally approved by the Commons despite a last-ditch resistance of some 20 anti-Marketeers.

The Final Boundaries

Eleven changes were made when the final boundaries were drawn. One of these changes was of name only — the proposed North of Scotland constituency was renamed Highlands and Islands. In terms of likely outcome, the two most significant of the 10 boundary revisions were in Cleveland and North London. Both seats (see Table 6 below) are now more vulnerable to capture by the Conservatives.

Electorates

Despite the efforts of those drawing up the boundaries, the electorates of the constituencies were far from uniform. Two seats (Glasgow and Kent West) had electorates over 550,000. At the opposite extreme, the Highlands & Islands seat, although vast in area, had only 279,521 electors (see Table 7).

The amalgamation of several Westminster constituencies into one Euroconstituency produced some unusual combinations: thus in North East London proletarian Bethnal Green and Bow is in the same constituency as suburban Chingford; in London South West, Richmond will share the same Euro MP as Lambeth Central or Vauxhall. The electors in some areas will be forgiven for experiencing some degree of confusion. Thus in the county of Leicestershire, the voters of Harborough find themselves in the Northamptonshire Euroconstituency while the voters of Blaby, Bosworth and Loughborough are in the East Midlands seat. But at the same time, the Leicestershire Euroconstituency includes Carlton, Newark and Rushcliffe — none of which are in the county of Leicester.

Despite the heterogeneity caused by the mixing of different types of seats, there are still many constituencies with pronounced characteristics in their electoral composition. Four such characteristics — the most mining seats, the most agricultural, the most middle-class and the seats with most voters from the New Commonwealth are given in Tables 8, 9, 10 and 11. The full details of the 78 Euroconstituencies are set out in Table 12.

TABLE 6

Euroconstituency	% majority as originally proposed*		Final % majority	
Bedfordshire	1.7	Con	2.8	Con
Cambridgeshire	10.2	Con	9.4	Con
Cleveland	16.8	Lab	6.9	Lab
Durham	28.7	Lab	38.1	Lab
Hertfordshire	4.3	Con	3.1	Con
Lincolnshire	8.5	Con	9.5	Con
London North	17.9	Lab	10.2	Lab
London North East	30.3	Lab	39.0	Lab
Lothians	10.3	Lab	10.9	Lab
South of Scotland	1.1	Lab	1.8	Lab

* i.e. the majority if the electors vote as they did in October 1974.

TABLE 7

6 lowest electorates

1	Highlands & Islands	279,521
2	South of Scotland	427,580
3	Essex South West	446,153
4	Strathclyde East	450,263
5	North East Scotland	453,495
6	East Midlands	453,865

6 highest electorates

1	Glasgow	581,986
2	Kent West	551,446
3	London North East	549,842
4	Isle of Wight — Hamp.	549,346
5	London East	545,897
6	Lancashire West	542,961

TABLE 8

The 8 most mining Euroconstituencies (over 5% in mining)

	Euroconstituency	av % mining
1	Yorkshire South	13.5
2	Durham	10.9
3	South East Wales	10.0
4	Yorkshire South West	10.0
5	Nottingham	9.7
6	Derbyshire	7.0
7	Northumbria	5.9
8	Staffordshire East	5.5

Electorates

TABLE 9

The 12 most rural Euroconstituencies (over 8% in agriculture)

	Euroconstituency	av % in agriculture
1	Highlands & Islands	17.0
2	Mid & West Wales	12.7
3	Lincolnshire	12.4
4	Devon	12.0
5	South of Scotland	11.7
6	North Wales	11.6
7	North East Scotland	10.8
8	Norfolk	10.0
9	Hereford & Worcester	9.5
10	Salop & Staffs	8.8
11	Cornwall & Plymouth	8.6
12	Suffolk	8.5

TABLE 10

The 15 most middle-class Euroconstituencies (over 15% middle-class)

	Euroconstituency	% middle-class
1	Surrey	22.0
2	Thames Valley	18.3
3	London North West	18.2
4	Sussex West	17.0
5	London Central	17.0
6	Hertfordshire	16.8
7	London South	16.5
8	Devon	16.2
9	Sussex East	15.8
10	Wessex	15.6
11	London South East	15.4
12	Essex South West	15.2
13	Cheshire East	15.1
14	West Kent	15.1
15	Essex North East	15.0

TABLE 11

The 9 constituencies with the greatest percentage of voters from the New Commonwealth (over 5%)

	Euroconstituency	% New Commonwealth
1	London North	12.6
2	Birmingham South	12.5
3	London North East	11.0
4	London South Inner	9.1
5	London North West	9.0
6	London South West	8.7
7	London Central	7.9
8	London West	7.6
9	Midlands West	6.8

TABLE 12
EUROCONSTITUENCIES*

NORTHUMBRIA
Berwick-on-Tweed (Lib); Blyth (Lab); Hexham (Con); Morpeth (Lab); Newcastle Central (Lab); Newcastle East (Lab); Newcastle North (Con); Newcastle West (Lab); Wallsend (Lab)
Electorate: 508,123   *Probable outcome:* LABOUR

SOUTH TYNE & WEAR
Blaydon (Lab); Gateshead East (Lab); Gateshead West (Lab); Jarrow (Lab); South Shields (Lab); Sunderland North (Lab); Sunderland South (Lab); Tynemouth (Con)
Electorate: 506,877   *Probable outcome:* LABOUR

CUMBRIA
Barrow-in-Furness (Lab); Carlisle (Lab); Lancaster (Con); Morecambe and Lonsdale (Con); Penrith and the Borders (Con); Westmoreland (Con); Whitehaven (Lab); Workington (Lab); Fylde North (Con)
Electorate 515,211   *Probable outcome:* CONSERVATIVE

DURHAM
Bishop Auckland (Lab); Chester-le-Street (Lab); Consett (Lab); Darlington (Lab); Durham (Lab); Houghton-le-Spring (Lab); Durham North West (Lab); Easington (Lab)
Electorate: 522,485   *Probable outcome:* LABOUR

* Results of October 1974 for the Westminster constituencies are in parentheses. By-election changes are excluded.

Electorates

TABLE 12 — *cont.*

CLEVELAND
Cleveland and Whitby (Con); Richmond (Con); Hartlepool (Lab);
Middlesbrough (Lab); Redcar (Lab); Stockton (Lab); Thornaby
(Lab); Scarborough (Con)
Electorate: 516,892   *Probable outcome:* LABOUR (marginal)

YORKSHIRE NORTH
Barkston Ash (Con); Harrogate (Con); Goole (Lab); Ripon
(Con); Skipton (Con); Thirsk & Malton (Con); York (Lab)
Electorate: 456,841   *Probable outcome:* CONSERVATIVE

HUMBERSIDE
Bridlington (Con); Brigg and Scunthorpe (Lab); Haltemprice
(Con); Howden (Con); Hull Central (Lab); Hull East (Lab);
Hull West (Lab)
Electorate: 492,053   *Probable outcome:* LABOUR (marginal)

LANCASHIRE CENTRAL
Blackpool North (Con); Blackpool South (Con); Chorley (Lab);
Westhoughton (Lab); Wigan (Lab); Preston North (Lab); Preston
South (Lab); Fylde South (Con)
Electorate: 516,507   *Probable outcome:* LABOUR (marginal)

LANCASHIRE EAST
Accrington (Lab); Blackburn (Lab); Burnley (Lab); Clitheroe
(Con); Darwen (Con); Heywood & Royton (Lab); Nelson &
Colne (Lab); Rossendale (Lab)
Electorate: 457,072   *Probable outcome:* LABOUR (marginal)

YORKSHIRE WEST
Bradford North (Lab); Bradford South (Lab); Bradford West
(Lab); Brighouse & Spenborough (Lab); Halifax (Lab); Keighley
(Lab); Shipley (Con); Sowerby (Lab)
Electorate: 481,672   *Probable outcome:* LABOUR

LEEDS
Batley and Morley (Lab); Leeds East (Lab); Leeds North East
(Con); Leeds South (Lab); Leeds South East (Lab); Leeds West
(Lab); Pudsey (Con)
Electorate: 481,795   *Probable outcome:* LABOUR

LIVERPOOL
Bootle (Lab); Liverpool Edgehill (Lab); Liverpool Garston (Lab);
Liverpool Kirkdale (Lab); Liverpool Scotland Exchange (Lab);
Liverpool Toxteth (Lab); Liverpool Walton (Lab); Liverpool

175

TABLE 12 — *cont.*

Wavertree (Con); Liverpool West Derby (Lab)
Electorate: 483,041   *Probable outcome:* LABOUR

LANCASHIRE WEST
  Crosby (Con); Huyton (Lab); Ince (Lab); Ormskirk (Lab); St.
  Helens (Lab); Southport (Con); Widnes (Lab)
Electorate: 542,961   *Probable outcome:* LABOUR

GREATER MANCHESTER WEST
  Bolton East (Lab); Bolton West (Lab); Eccles (Lab); Farnworth
  (Lab); Leigh (Lab); Altrincham & Sale (Con); Salford East (Lab);
  Salford West (Lab); Stretford (Con)
Electorate: 532,026   *Probable outcome:* LABOUR

GREATER MANCHESTER SOUTH
  Manchester Ardwick (Lab); Manchester Blackley (Lab);
  Manchester Central (Lab); Manchester Moss Side (Lab);
  Manchester Openshaw (Lab); Manchester Withington (Con);
  Manchester Wythenshawe (Lab); Cheadle (Con); Stockport North
  (Lab); Stockport South (Lab)
Electorate: 526,031   *Probable outcome:* LABOUR

GREATER MANCHESTER NORTH
  Ashton-under-Lyne (Lab); Bury & Radcliffe (Lab); Middleton &
  Prestwich (Lab); Oldham East (Lab); Oldham West (Lab);
  Rochdale (Lib); Stalybridge & Hyde (Lab); Manchester Gorton
  (Lab)
Electorate: 502,977   *Probable outcome:* LABOUR

YORKSHIRE SOUTH WEST
  Hemsworth (Lab); Pontefract & Castleford (Lab); Colne Valley
  (Lib); Dewsbury (Lab); Huddersfield East (Lab); Huddersfield
  West (Lab); Normanton (Lab); Wakefield (Lab)
Electorate: 484,753   *Probable outcome:* LABOUR

YORKSHIRE SOUTH
  Dearne Valley (Lab); Doncaster (Lab); Don Valley (Lab);
  Barnsley (Lab); Penistone (Lab); Rotherham (Lab); Rother
  Valley (Lab)
Electorate: 508,179   *Probable outcome:* LABOUR

CHESHIRE WEST
  Bebington & Ellesmere Port (Lab); Birkenhead (Lab);
  Chester (Con); Nantwich (Con); Wallasey (Con); The Wirral

Electorates

TABLE 12 — *cont.*

(Con)
Electorate: 493,563   *Probable outcome:* CONSERVATIVE

CHESHIRE EAST
Warrington (Lab); Newton (Lab); Runcorn (Con); Crewe (Lab); Hazel Grove (Con); Knutsford (Con); Macclesfield (Con)
Electorate: 473,896   *Probable outcome:* CONSERVATIVE

DERBYSHIRE
Belper (Lab); Bolsover (Lab); Derbyshire South East (Lab); Derby North (Lab); Derby South (Lab); High Peak (Con); Ilkeston (Lab); Derbyshire West (Con)
Electorate: 514,946   *Probable outcome:* LABOUR

SHEFFIELD
Chesterfield (Lab); Derbyshire North East (Lab); Sheffield Attercliffe (Lab); Sheffield Brightside (Lab); Sheffield Hallam (Con); Sheffield Heeley (Lab); Sheffield Hillsborough (Lab); Sheffield Park (Lab)
Electorate: 518,083   *Probable outcome:* LABOUR

NOTTINGHAM
Ashfield (Lab); Bassetlaw (Lab); Beeston (Con); Mansfield (Lab); Nottingham East (Lab); Nottingham North (Lab); Nottingham West (Lab)
Electorate: 497,987   *Probable outcome:* LABOUR

LINCOLNSHIRE
Gainsborough (Con); Grantham (Con); Grimsby (Lab); Holland & Boston (Con); Lincoln (Lab); Rutland and Stamford (Con)
Electorate: 514,586   *Probable outcome:* CONSERVATIVE

SALOP AND STAFFORDSHIRE
Newcastle-under-Lyme (Lab); Stafford & Stone (Con); Ludlow (Con); Oswestry (Con); Shrewsbury (Con); Staffordshire South West (Con); The Wrekin (Lab)
Electorate: 460,464   *Probable outcome:* CONSERVATIVE

STAFFORDSHIRE EAST
Burton (Con); Cannock (Lab); Leek (Con); Lichfield & Tamworth (Lab); Stoke Central (Lab); Stoke North (Lab); Stoke South (Lab)
Electorate: 491,677   *Probable outcome:* LABOUR

TABLE 12 — *cont.*

MIDLANDS WEST
Dudley East (Lab); Dudley West (Lab); Walsall North (Lab);
Walsall South (Lab); Halesowen and Stourbridge (Con); Wolver-
hampton North East (Lab); Wolverhampton South East (Lab)
Wolverhampton South West (Con)
Electorate 536,927   *Probable outcome:* LABOUR

BIRMINGHAM NORTH
West Bromwich East (Lab); Birmingham Erdington (Lab); West
Bromwich West (Lab); Warley East (Lab); Birmingham Perry Barr
(Lab); Warley West (Lab); Aldridge-Brownhills (Lab);
Birmingham Stechford (Lab); Sutton Coldfield (Con)
Electorate: 539,820   *Probable outcome:* LABOUR

BIRMINGHAM SOUTH
Birmingham Hall Green (Con); Birmingham Northfields (Lab);
Birmingham Selly Oak (Lab); Birmingham Edgbaston (Con);
Birmingham Handsworth (Lab); Birmingham Ladywood (Lab);
Birmingham Small Heath (Lab); Birmingham Sparkbrook (Lab);
Birmingham Yardley (Lab)
Electorate: 523,574   *Probable outcome:* LABOUR

MIDLANDS EAST
Blaby (Con); Bosworth (Con); Loughborough (Lab); Meriden
(Lab); Nuneaton (Lab); Rugby (Lab)
Electorate: 453,865   *Probable outcome:* LABOUR (marginal)

LEICESTERSHIRE
Carlton (Con); Melton (Con); Newark (Lab); Rushcliffe (Con);
Leicester East (Lab); Leicester South (Lab); Leicester West (Lab)
Electorate: 490,222   *Probable outcome:* CONSERVATIVE

CAMBRIDGESHIRE
Wellingborough (Con); Peterborough (Lab); Cambridge (Con);
Cambridgeshire (Con); Huntingdonshire (Con); Isle of Ely (Lib)
Electorate: 456,822   *Probable outcome:* CONSERVATIVE

NORFOLK
Norfolk North (Con); Norfolk North West (Con); Norwich North
(Lab); Norwich South (Lab); Norfolk South (Con); Norfolk
South West (Con); Yarmouth (Con)
Electorate: 475,430   *Probable outcome:* CONSERVATIVE

SUFFOLK
Bury St. Edmunds (Con); Eye (Con); Harwich (Con); Ipswich

TABLE 12 — *cont.*

(Lab); Lowestoft (Con); Sudbury & Woodbridge (Con)
Electorate: 490,525   *Probable outcome:* CONSERVATIVE

HEREFORD & WORCESTER
Bromsgrove & Redditch (Con); Hereford (Con); Kidderminster
(Con); Leominster (Con); Worcestershire South (Con); Worcester
(Con); Gloucestershire West (Lab)
Electorate: 484,374   *Probable outcome:* CONSERVATIVE

COTSWOLDS
Cheltenham (Con); Cirencester & Tewkesbury (Con); Gloucester
(Con); Banbury (Con); Mid-Oxfordshire (Con); Oxford (Con);
Stroud (Con)
Electorate: 479,431   *Probable outcome:* CONSERVATIVE

MIDLANDS CENTRAL
Coventry North East (Lab); Coventry North West (Lab);
Coventry South East (Lab); Coventry South West (Lab); Solihull
(Con); Stratford-on-Avon (Con); Warwick & Leamington (Con)
Electorate: 461,963   *Probable outcome:* CONSERVATIVE

NORTHAMPTONSHIRE
Daventry (Con); Northampton North (Lab); Northampton
South (Con); Harborough (Con); Kettering (Lab); Aylesbury
(Con); Buckingham (Con)
Electorate: 474,964   *Probable outcome:* CONSERVATIVE

BEDFORD
Hemel Hempstead (Lab); Luton East (Lab); Luton West (Lab);
Hitchin (Con); Bedfordshire South (Con); Bedford (Con); Mid-
Bedfordshire (Con)
Electorate: 481,945   *Probable outcome:* CONSERVATIVE

HERTFORDSHIRE
Hertfordshire East (Con); Hertford & Stevenage (Lab); St. Albans
(Con); Hertfordshire South West (Con); Watford (Lab); Welwyn
& Hatfield (Lab); Hertfordshire South (Con)
Electorate: 504,433   *Probable outcome:* CONSERVATIVE

ESSEX SOUTH WEST
Basildon (Lab); Brentwood & Ongar (Con); Chelmsford (Con);
Epping Forest (Con); Harlow (Lab); Thurrock (Lab)
Electorate: 446,153   *Probable outcome:* LABOUR (marginal)

TABLE 12 — *cont.*

ESSEX NORTH EAST
Braintree (Con); Colchester (Con); Maldon (Con); Saffron Walden (Con); Essex South East (Con); Southend East (Con); Southend West (Con)
Electorate: 472,132   *Probable outcome:* CONSERVATIVE

BRISTOL
Bristol North East (Lab); Bristol North West (Lab); Bristol South (Lab); Bristol South East (Lab); Bristol West (Con); Kingswood (Lab); Gloucestershire South (Con); Chippenham (Con)
Electorate: 512,411   *Probable outcome:* LABOUR (marginal)

UPPER THAMES
Abingdon (Con); Devizes (Con); Henley (Con); Reading South (Con); Newbury (Con); Swindon (Lab); Reading North (Con)
Electorate: 499,672   *Probable outcome:* CONSERVATIVE

THAMES VALLEY
Wokingham (Con); Beaconsfield (Con); Spelthorne (Con); Chesham & Amersham (Con); Eton & Slough (Lab); Windsor & Maidenhead (Con); Wycombe (Con)
Electorate: 497,150   *Probable outcome:* CONSERVATIVE

CORNWALL & PLYMOUTH
Bodmin (Con); Falmouth & Camborne (Con); Cornwall North (Lib); Plymouth Devonport (Lab); Plymouth Drake (Con); Plymouth Sutton (Con); St. Ives (Con); Truro (Lib)
Electorate: 464,188   *Probable outcome:* CONSERVATIVE

DEVON
Exeter (Con); Honiton (Con); Tiverton (Con); Totnes (Con); Torbay (Con); Devon West (Con); Devon North (Lib)
Electorate: 507,349   *Probable outcome:* CONSERVATIVE

SOMERSET
Bath (Con); Bridgwater (Con); Somerset North (Con); Taunton (Con); Wells (Con); Weston-super-Mare (Con); Yeovil (Con)
Electorate: 514,447   *Probable outcome:* CONSERVATIVE

WESSEX
Bournemouth East (Con); Bournemouth West (Con); Christchurch & Lymington (Con); Westbury (Con); Dorset North (Con); Poole (Con); Dorset South (Con); Dorset West (Con)
Electorate: 525,705   *Probable outcome:* CONSERVATIVE

HAMPSHIRE WEST
Basingstoke (Con); Eastleigh (Con); New Forest (Con); Salisbury
(Con); Southampton Itchen (Lab); Southampton Test (Lab);
Winchester (Con)
Electorate: 542,088   *Probable outcome:* CONSERVATIVE

ISLE OF WIGHT & HAMPSHIRE EAST
Aldershot (Con); Fareham (Con); Gosport (Con); Isle of Wight
(Lib); Portsmouth North (Lab); Portsmouth South (Con);
Farnham (Con); Petersfield (Con)
Electorate: 549,346   *Probable outcome:* CONSERVATIVE

SURREY
Chertsey & Walton (Con); Dorking (Con); Surrey North West
(Con); Epsom & Ewell (Con); Esher (Con); Guildford (Con);
Reigate (Con); Woking (Con)
Electorate: 536,402   *Probable outcome:* CONSERVATIVE

SUSSEX WEST
Arundel (Con); Chichester (Con); Havant & Waterloo (Con);
Horsham & Crawley (Con); Mid-Sussex (Con); Shoreham (Con);
Worthing (Con)
Electorate: 521,685   *Probable outcome:* CONSERVATIVE

SUSSEX EAST
Brighton Kemptown (Con); Brighton Pavilion (Con); Eastbourne
(Con); East Grinstead (Con); Hastings (Con); Hove (Con); Lewes
(Con); Rye (Con)
Electorate: 527,368   *Probable outcome:* CONSERVATIVE

KENT WEST
Dartford (Lab); Gillingham (Con); Gravesend (Lab); Surrey East
(Con); Rochester & Chatham (Lab); Sevenoaks (Con); Tonbridge
& Walling (Con); Tunbridge Wells (Con)
Electorate: 551,446   *Probable outcome:* CONSERVATIVE

KENT EAST
Ashford (Con); Canterbury (Con); Dover & Deal (Con);
Faversham (Con); Folkestone & Hythe (Con); Maidstone (Con);
Thanet East (Con); Thanet West (Con)
Electorate: 539,403   *Probable outcome:* CONSERVATIVE

LONDON WEST
Acton (Con); Ealing North (Lab); Southall (Lab); Brent &
Isleworth (Con); Hayes & Harlington (Lab); Ruislip-

Northwood (Con); Uxbridge (Con); Feltham & Heston (Lab)
Electorate: 521,309   *Probable outcome:* LABOUR (marginal)

LONDON NORTH WEST
   Chipping Barnet (Con); Hendon North (Con); Hendon South
   (Con); Brent East (Lab); Brent North (Con); Brent South (Lab);
   Harrow Central (Con); Harrow East (Con); Harrow West (Con)
Electorate: 506,763   *Probable outcome:* CONSERVATIVE

LONDON CENTRAL
   Hampstead (Con); Holborn & St. Pancras South (Lab); St. Pancras
   North (Lab); City of London & Westminster (Con); Paddington
   (Lab); St. Marylebone (Con); Fulham (Lab); Chelsea (Con);
   Kensington (Con); Hammersmith North (Lab)
Electorate: 535,451   *Probable outcome:* CONSERVATIVE

LONDON NORTH
   Edmonton (Lab); Enfield North (Lab); Islington North (Lab);
   Hornsey (Con); Tottenham (Lab); Wood Green (Lab); Islington
   Central (Lab); Islington South & Finsbury (Lab); Southgate
   (Con)
Electorate: 540,874   *Probable outcome:* LABOUR

LONDON NORTH EAST
   Hackney Central (Lab); Hackney North & Stoke Newington
   (Lab); Bethnal Green & Bow (Lab); Stepney & Poplar (Lab);
   Newham North West (Lab); Newham South (Lab); Chingford
   (Con); Leyton (Lab); Walthamstow (Lab); Hackney South &
   Shoreditch (Lab)
Electorate: 549,842   *Probable outcome:* LABOUR

LONDON EAST
   Barking (Lab); Dagenham (Lab); Hornchurch (Lab); Romford
   (Con); Upminster (Con); Newham North East (Lab); Ilford North
   (Lab); Ilford South (Lab); Wanstead & Woodford (Con)
Electorate: 545,897   *Probable outcome:* LABOUR

LONDON SOUTH WEST
   Lambeth Central (Lab); Vauxhall (Lab); Kingston (Con);
   Surbiton (Con); Richmond (Con); Twickenham (Con); Battersea
   North (Lab); Battersea South (Lab); Putney (Lab); Tooting (Lab)
Electorate: 538,310   *Probable outcome:* LABOUR (marginal)

LONDON SOUTH
   Croydon Central (Con); Croydon North East (Con); Croydon
   North West (Con); Croydon South (Con); Mitcham & Morden

(Lab); Wimbledon (Con); Sutton & Cheam (Con); Carshalton
(Con)
Electorate: 503,737   *Probable outcome:* CONSERVATIVE

LONDON SOUTH INNER
Greenwich (Lab); Norwood (Lab); Streatham (Con); Deptford
(Lab); Lewisham East (Lab); Lewisham West (Lab); Bermondsey
(Lab); Dulwich (Lab); Peckham (Lab)
Electorate: 541,405   *Probable outcome:* LABOUR

LONDON SOUTH EAST
Bexleyheath (Con); Erith & Crayford (Lab); Sidcup (Con);
Beckenham (Con); Chislehurst (Con); Orpington (Con);
Ravensbourne (Con); Woolwich East (Lab); Woolwich West
(Lab)
Electorate: 495,846   *Probable outcome:* CONSERVATIVE

NORTH WALES
Anglesey (Lab); Caernarvon (PC); Conway (Con); Denbigh
(Con); Flint East (Lab); Merioneth (PC); Montgomeryshire (Lib);
Flint West (Con); Wrexham (Lab)
Electorate: 471,656   *Probable outcome:* LABOUR

MID & WEST WALES
Brecon & Radnor (Lab); Cardigan (Lib); Carmarthen (PC); Gower
(Lab); Llanelli (Lab); Pembroke (Con); Swansea East (Lab);
Swansea West (Lab)
Electorate: 475,073   *Probable outcome:* LABOUR

SOUTH EAST WALES
Aberdare (Lab); Abertillery (Lab); Bedwellty (Lab); Caerphilly
(Lab); Ebbw Vale (Lab); Merthyr Tydfil (Lab); Monmouth (Con);
Newport (Lab); Pontypool (Lab); Rhondda (Lab)
Electorate: 539,609   *Probable outcome:* LABOUR

SOUTH WALES
Aberavon (Lab); Barry (Con); Cardiff North (Con); Cardiff North
West (Con); Cardiff South East (Lab); Cardiff West (Lab);
Ogmore (Lab); Pontypridd (Lab); Neath (Lab)
Electorate: 521,946   *Probable outcome:* LABOUR

HIGHLANDS & ISLANDS
Orkney & Shetlands (Lib); Western Isles (SNP); Caithness &
Sutherland (Lab); Ross & Cromarty (Con); Inverness (Lib);
Moray & Nairn (SNP); Banff (SNP); Argyll (SNP)
Electorate: 279,521   *Probable outcome:* SNP

TABLE 12 — *cont.*

NORTH EAST SCOTLAND
   Aberdeenshire East (SNP); Aberdeenshire West (Con); Aberdeen
   North (Lab); Aberdeen South (Con); Angus North & Mearns
   (Con); Angus South (SNP); Dundee East (SNP); Dundee West
   (Lab)
Electorate: 453,495   *Probable outcome:* SNP

MID SCOTLAND & FIFE
   Fife Central (Lab); Dunfermline (Lab); Fife East (Con);
   Kirkcaldy (Lab); Stirlingshire East & Clackmannan (SNP);
   Stirlingshire West (Lab); Stirling, Falkirk & Grangemouth (Lab);
   Kinross & West Perthshire (Con); Perth & East Perthshire (SNP)
Electorate: 509,287   *Probable outcome:* SNP (marginal)

LOTHIANS
   Midlothian (Lab); West Lothian (Lab); Edinburgh Central (Lab);
   Edinburgh East (Lab); Edinburgh Leith (Lab); Edinburgh North
   (Con); Edinburgh Pentlands (Con); Edinburgh South (Con);
   Edinburgh West (Con)
Electorate: 515,434   *Probable outcome:* LABOUR

SOUTH OF SCOTLAND
   Roxburgh, Selkirk & Peebles (Lib); Dumfries (Con); Galloway
   (SNP); Ayrshire South (Lab); Ayr (Con); Ayrshire Central (Lab);
   Lanark (Lab); Berwick & East Lothian (Lab)
Electorate: 427,580   *Probable outcome:* LABOUR (marginal)

GLASGOW
   Glasgow Cathcart (Con); Glasgow Central (Lab); Glasgow
   Craigton (Lab); Glasgow Garscadden (Lab); Glasgow Govan
   (Lab); Glasgow Hillhead (Con); Glasgow Kelvingrove (Lab);
   Glasgow Maryhill (Lab); Glasgow Pollok (Lab); Glasgow Provan
   (Lab); Glasgow Queens Park (Lab); Glasgow Shettleston (Lab);
   Glasgow Springburn (Lab)
Electorate: 581,986   *Probable outcome:* LABOUR

STRATHCLYDE WEST
   Renfrewshire East (Con); Renfrewshire West (Lab); Greenock &
   Port Glasgow (Lab); Paisley (Lab); Dunbartonshire East (SNP);
   Dunbartonshire Central (Lab); Dunbartonshire West (Lab);
   Ayrshire North & Bute (Lab)
Electorate: 469,226   *Probable outcome:* LABOUR

STRATHCLYDE EAST
   Bothwell (Lab); East Kilbride (Lab); Kilmarnock (Lab); Hamilton

TABLE 12 – *cont.*

(Lab); Lanarkshire North (Lab); Rutherglen (Lab); Coatbridge & Airdrie (Lab); Morthwell & Wishaw (Lab)
Electorate: 450,263   *Probable outcome:* LABOUR

The base voting statistics in these Euroconstituencies, based on the voting in October 1974, are set out in Table 13. As with every election, there are the safe seats which are highly unlikely to change hands, unless turnout drops very significantly (see p 191). Table 14 sets out the 8 Conservative seats that would fall on a 7½% or more swing from Conservative to their nearest challenger. Table 15 sets out the Labour seats vulnerable only on swings over 7½%.

TABLE 13

ENGLAND

	Con	Lab	Lib	Others
Northumbria	29.5	46.5	18.4	5.6
South Tyne & Wear	28.2	55.7	15.9	0.2
Cumbria	43.8	37.4	18.7	0.1
Durham	22.6	60.7	16.8	—
Cleveland	38.3	45.2	16.3	0.2
Yorkshire North	45.2	31.3	22.9	0.7
Humberside	36.6	39.7	23.4	0.3
Lancashire Central	40.4	42.1	17.2	0.3
Lancashire East	37.1	43.4	18.7	0.8
Yorkshire West	36.7	44.6	18.1	0.7
Leeds	32.1	46.1	21.6	0.2
Liverpool	31.5	55.9	12.2	0.4
Lancashire West	33.9	49.5	16.6	—
Greater Manchester West	34.2	47.5	17.6	0.7
Greater Manchester South	35.2	45.6	18.7	0.4
Greater Manchester North	32.0	48.0	19.4	0.7
Yorkshire South West	23.4	55.0	21.0	0.6
Yorkshire South	21.2	63.1	15.7	—
Cheshire West	42.6	39.3	17.9	0.2
Cheshire East	40.6	37.6	21.7	0.1
Derbyshire	35.5	46.7	17.6	0.3

TABLE 13 — *cont.*

	Con	Lab	Lib	Others
Sheffield	27.0	54.3	15.6	3.1
Nottingham	31.4	52.1	15.7	0.8
Lincolnshire	41.7	32.2	22.5	3.7
Salop & Staffs	43.2	36.1	20.6	0.2
Staffordshire East	35.6	50.0	14.5	—
Midlands West	33.2	49.3	15.3	2.2
Birmingham North	34.4	48.6	15.4	1.7
Birmingham South	35.5	49.0	14.6	1.0
Midlands East	37.5	43.7	18.4	0.4
Leicestershire	42.3	38.7	16.6	2.4
Cambridgeshire	42.6	33.2	23.9	0.3
Norfolk	43.3	38.9	17.7	0.1
Suffolk	45.7	34.2	20.1	—
Hereford & Worcester	44.0	31.1	24.9	—
Cotswolds	45.2	32.2	22.1	0.4
Midlands Central	40.5	39.0	19.9	0.6
Northamptonshire	42.8	36.7	20.5	—
Bedford	41.3	38.6	20.0	0.1
Hertfordshire	40.7	37.7	21.1	0.5
Essex South West	35.6	40.7	23.5	0.2
Bristol	37.5	39.9	22.0	0.6
Upper Thames	42.2	31.2	26.4	0.2
Thames Valley	45.0	30.4	23.4	1.2
Cornwall & Plymouth	43.2	27.0	28.9	0.9
Devon	45.8	20.1	34.0	0.1
Somerset	43.8	28.6	26.9	0.6
Wessex	48.7	23.5	27.6	0.2
Hampshire West	43.2	32.8	23.8	0.2
Wight & Hampshire	46.0	23.9	29.0	1.1
Surrey	51.1	23.5	25.0	0.4
Sussex West	50.8	22.7	26.2	0.3
Sussex East	51.5	24.4	24.0	0.1
Kent West	43.5	33.8	21.6	1.1
Kent East	45.3	31.3	22.9	0.5
London West	39.4	44.3	14.9	1.4
North West	43.3	37.9	17.1	1.7
Central	42.5	42.4	14.1	1.0
North	34.9	45.1	16.0	4.0
North East	21.4	60.4	13.9	4.3
East	34.6	47.1	16.5	1.8
South West	38.3	41.2	19.5	1.0
South	45.2	33.3	20.9	0.6
South Inner	29.6	54.4	14.3	1.7
South East	42.5	35.6	21.4	0.5

Electorates

TABLE 13 — *cont.*

WALES

	Con	Lab	Lib	PC	Others
North Wales	29.2	36.0	21.0	13.8	—
Mid & West Wales	22.5	47.5	16.5	13.4	0.1
South East Wales	17.3	62.2	10.3	9.5	0.7
South Wales	27.2	50.6	15.1	7.0	0.1

SCOTLAND

	Con	Lab	Lib	SNP	Others
Highlands & Islands	28.5	16.2	17.7	37.5	0.1
North East Scotland	28.3	27.5	9.7	34.4	0.1
Mid Scotland & Fife	22.4	34.3	5.6	37.5	0.3
Lothians	25.8	36.7	8.9	28.5	0.1
South of Scotland	31.5	33.3	11.4	23.8	—
Glasgow	20.2	49.1	4.2	26.2	0.3
Strathclyde West	25.7	36.2	8.9	28.3	0.9
Strathclyde East	18.1	46.3	5.0	30.3	0.3

TABLE 14

The 8 Conservative safe seats

Euroconstituency	% majority	Swing needed	Challenger
Sussex East	27.1	13.6	Labour
Surrey	26.1	13.1	Liberal
Sussex West	24.6	12.3	Liberal
Wessex	21.1	10.6	Liberal
Isle of Wight & Hampshire	17.0	8.5	Liberal
Somerset	15.2	7.6	Labour
Cornwall & Plymouth	14.3	7.2	Liberal
Devon	11.8	5.9	Liberal

187

TABLE 15

The 18 Labour safe seats

Euroconstituency	% majority	Swing needed	Challenger
South East Wales	44.8	22.4	Con
Yorkshire South	41.9	21.0	Con
London North East	39.0	19.5	Con
Durham	38.1	19.1	Con
Yorkshire South West	31.6	15.8	Con
Glasgow	28.9	14.5	SNP
Strathclyde East	28.2	14.1	SNP
South Tyne & Wear	27.5	13.8	Con
Sheffield	27.3	13.7	Con
Mid & West Wales	25.0	12.5	Con
London South Inner	24.8	12.4	Con
Liverpool	24.3	12.2	Con
South Wales	23.5	11.7	Con
Nottingham	20.8	10.4	Con
Northumbria	17.0	8.5	Con
Midlands West	16.1	8.1	Con
Greater Manchester North	16.0	8.0	Con
Lancashire West	15.6	7.8	Con

TABLE 16

The key marginals: Labour with Conservative nearest challengers

Euroconstituency	% majority	Swing needed
Staffordshire East	14.4	7.2
Birmingham North	14.2	7.1
Leeds	13.9	7.0
Birmingham South	13.5	6.8
Greater Manchester West	13.3	6.7
London East	12.4	6.2
Derbyshire	11.2	5.6
Greater Manchester South	10.4	5.2
London North	10.2	5.1
Yorkshire West	7.9	4.0
Cleveland	6.9	3.5
North Wales	6.9	3.5
Lancashire East	6.2	3.1
Midlands East	6.2	3.1
Essex South West	5.1	2.6

Electorates

TABLE 16 — *cont.*

Euroconstituency	% majority	swing needed
London West	4.9	2.5
Humberside	3.1	1.6
London South West	2.9	1.5
Bristol	2.4	1.2
South of Scotland	1.8	0.9
Lancashire Central	1.7	0.9

TABLE 17

The key marginals: Conservative with Labour nearest challenger (all seats vulnerable on a 7.5% swing to Labour from October 1974 figures)

Euroconstituency	% majority	Swing needed
Thames Valley	14.6	7.3
Kent East	14.0	7.0
Yorkshire North	14.0	7.0
Essex North East	13.8	6.9
Cotswolds	13.0	6.5
Hereford & Worcester	12.8	6.4
London South	12.0	6.0
Suffolk	11.5	5.8
Upper Thames	11.0	5.5
Hampshire West	10.5	5.3
Kent West	9.8	4.9
Lincolnshire	9.5	4.8
Cambridgeshire	9.4	4.7
Salop and Staffs	7.1	3.6
London South East	6.8	3.4
Cumbria	6.5	3.3
Northamptonshire	6.2	3.1
London North West	5.4	2.7
Norfolk	4.4	2.2
Leicestershire	3.6	1.8
Cheshire West	3.2	1.6
Hertfordshire	3.1	1.6
Cheshire East	3.1	1.6
Bedford	2.8	1.4
Midlands Central	1.5	0.8
London Central	0.1	0.1

The Voting: Analysis and Prospects

The Battle for Scotland

North of the Border there will be a crucial battle to see if the Scottish Nationalists can secure representation in the European Parliament. The seats in which the SNP polled best are set out in order in Table 18. The vital Scottish marginals are set out in Table 19.

TABLE 18

		% SNP Oct. '74
1	Highlands & Islands	37.5
2	Mid-Scotland & Fife	37.5
3	North East Scotland	34.4
4	Strathclyde East	30.3
5	Lothians	28.5
6	Strathclyde West	28.3
7	Glasgow	26.2
8	South of Scotland	23.8

TABLE 19

The key marginals: the battle for Scotland

SNP SEATS

Euroconstituency	% majority	Swing needed	Challenger
Highlands & Islands	12.4	7.2	Con
Mid Scotland & Fife	11.9	6.0	Lab
North East Scotland	0.8	0.4	Con

SEATS WHERE SNP CHALLENING			Held by
Glasgow	28.9	14.5	Lab
Strathclyde East	28.2	14.1	Lab
Lothians	10.9	5.5	Lab
Strathclyde West	10.6	5.3	Lab

The other Scottish constituency (South of Scotland) is primarily a Labour/Conservative battle. A swing of 0.9% is needed for Conservatives to take the seat. The SNP polled 23.8% in October 1974.

190

The Liberals and the Direct Elections

As we saw in the Table on safe Conservative seats, there are no seats in which Liberals came second that could be classed as marginal. The closest Liberal challenger is in Devon (5.9% swing needed) and then Cornwall (7.2% swing needed). In the Isle of Wight and Hampshire — the fifth safest Conservative seat — an even larger swing would be needed for it to go Liberal.

Nonetheless, as Table 20 shows, Liberal strength in their best areas will be a significant pointer to their strength.

TABLE 20

The Liberal hopefuls		
The 10 Euroconstituencies in which the Liberals polled best in October 1974		
	Constituency	%
1	Devon	34.0
2	Isle of Wight & Hampshire	29.0
3	Cornwall & Plymouth	28.9
4	Wessex	27.6
5	Somerset	26.9
6	Upper Thames	26.4
7	Sussex West	26.2
8	Surrey	25.1
9	Hereford & Worcester	24.9
10	Essex North East	24.2

Turnout

Perhaps the most difficult area to forecast is likely turnout. Will the Euro-elections fail to attract the same turnout as a General Election? If they do, Labour could well suffer a massacre (see Table 23). If turnout is relatively normal, the constituencies listed in Tables 17 and 18 should show high turnout.

TABLE 21

Seats with highest turnout (based on October 1974)

1	South of Scotland	79.3
2	Somerset	78.4
3	Mid & West Wales	78.3
4	Bedford	77.9
5	East Midlands	77.8
6	Strathclyde East	77.7
7	Lancashire East	77.4
8	North Wales	77.3
9	Devon	77.2
10	Hertfordshire	77.0

TABLE 22

Seats with lowest turnout

1	London North East	57.4
2	London Central	59.1
3	London South Inner	62.9
4	London North	63.7
5	Birmingham South	65.4
6	Liverpool	65.8
7	London South West	66.8
8	Leeds	67.2
9	Greater Manchester South	68.8
10	Birmingham South	69.0

Turnout

TABLE 23

Projecting the outcome

Labour representation on given swing to or from Conservative*		Conservative representation on given swing to or from Labour*	
+ 10%	68	−10%	7
+ 7½%	67	− 7½%	8
+ 5%	57	− 5%	18
+ 4%	54	− 4%	21
+ 3%	50	− 3%	25
+ 2%	48	− 2%	27
+ 1%	43	− 1%	32
no swing	41	no swing	34
− 1%	39	+ 1%	36
− 2%	36	+ 2%	39
− 3%	34	+ 3%	41
− 4%	29	+ 4%	46
-- 5%	29	+ 5%	46
− 7½%	20	+ 7½%	55
−10%	16	+ 10%	59

− = swing to Con	− = swing to Lab
+ = swing to Lab	+ = swing to Con

* Assuming no change in Nationalist representation (i.e. SNP seats = 3.)

TABLE 24

The overall picture: Five possible outcomes

Electoral movement	Con	Lab	SNP	Lib	Ulster	Total
Small swing to Labour (2%)	27	48	3	0	3	81
No swing since October 1974	34	41	3	0	3	81
Small simultaneous swing to Con from Lab & SNP (2%)	40	36	2	0	3	81
Significant simultaneous swing to Con from Lab & SNP (5%)	47	29	2	0	3	81
Landslide to Con from Labour & SNP (10%), aided by heavy Labour abstentions	61	16	1	0	3	81